Poetic Adventures in Scotland with Seventy Poems

to James

Sally Evans

Sally Evans

at Nairn, September 2014

diehard publishers 2014

diehard at the Callander Press
91-93 Main Street
Callander
FK17 8BQ

e-book
Firewater Press 2013

cover photographs by Dominique Carton
paper book: the author
e-book: Glencoe

paper book: ISBN 978-0946230-90-7

Contents

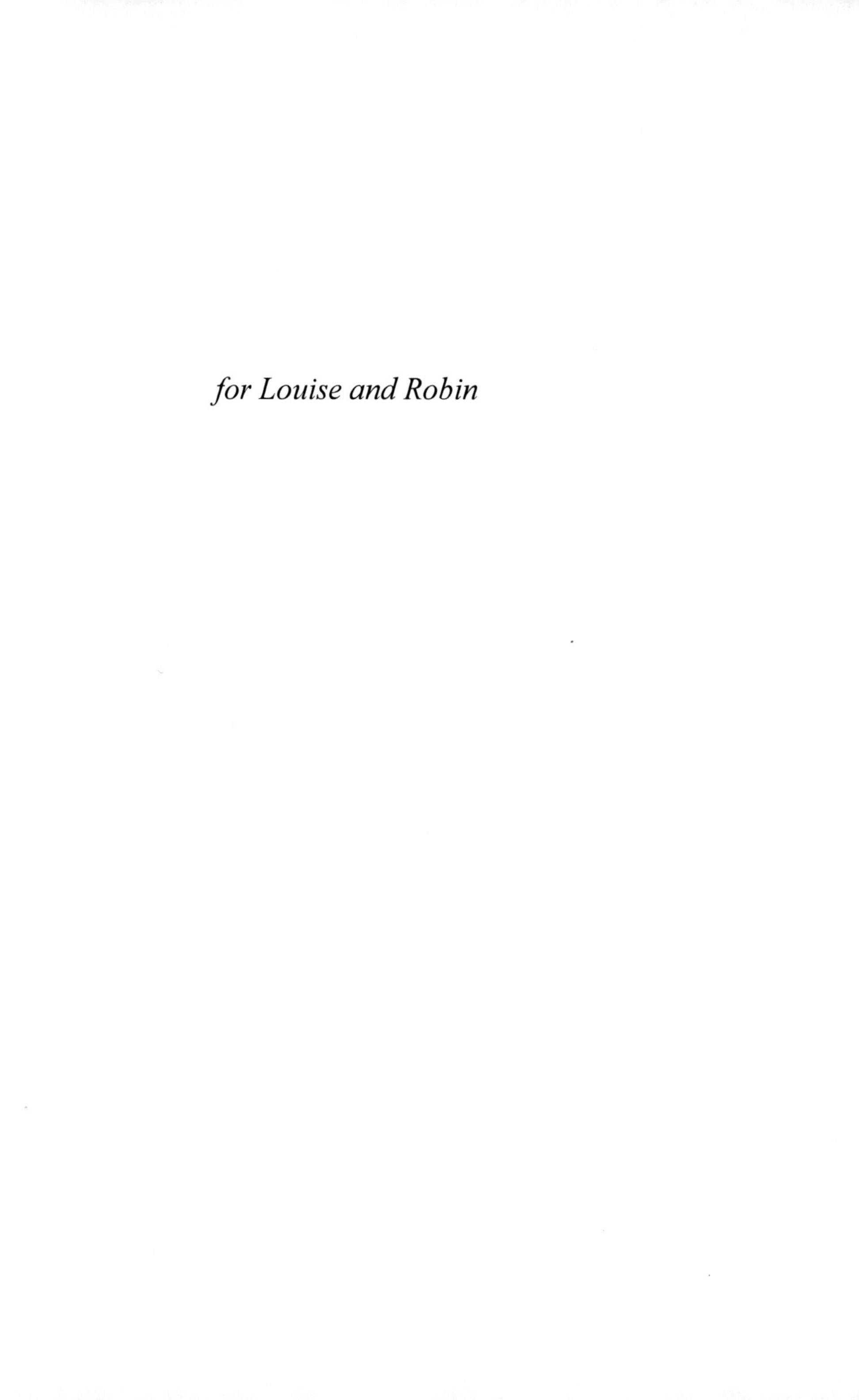

for Louise and Robin

In Scotland

I had read and written all my life, poems and novels, in the main unpublished, though a climate like today's would have made publication of some of this work more likely. An accidental removal to Scotland (late 1979), where my Welsh background undoubtedly contributed to my responding so strongly to the change, got me writing hard again. I met poets in Edinburgh, joined the original School of Poets, and went to many readings, most memorably those by Sorley Maclean.

Towards the end of this time I met Ian W King, and by 1987 Old Grindles Bookshop in Edinburgh was up and running.

This story really begins with the Sandy Bells. My then husband moved us to Edinburgh for a job in the University buildings in the lane behind this pub, where the taxi disgorged us on my first arrival in Edinburgh. It was a different country, a different world from the one I knew. Or the ones I knew, for I had moved about considerably, claiming (probably in this order) London, Newcastle, County Durham, Westmorland, Cardiff, North Wales, Nottingham and Milan as previous bases. But nothing had prepared me for living in Scotland.

My own work in Newcastle having inevitably been thrown into chaos, and with one then two young children, whose nanny had also been left in Newcastle, I soon found myself mesmerised by the company of a group of Scottish poets who largely revolved round the Sandy Bells.

Hamish Henderson and his dog were always at the centre of this group, while Sorley Maclean still regularly visited Edinburgh to read his extraordinary Gaelic poems, and Norman MacCaig reigned as Scotland's witty and exclusive unofficial makar. Male dominance was the rule in poetry.

Reading Scottish poetry, and beginning my still incomplete affair with the Gaelic language, I soon went back to verse writing, from this new perspective.

I was aware of difficulties and some opposition, but within a reasonable time Duncan Glen, Joy Hendry and others were publishing some of my poems.

Silly Question to a Poet feels very English, what with Hardy and the oak trees. It made it into in *Woven by Women*, a special issue of Chapman. Later it was included in an anthology of Scottish Women's Poetry published by Edinburgh University Press. Owing to a fairly typical poetic oversight, I only found out about this fifteen years after the book was published. In so far as I did hear this question asked of a poet, I was already benefiting from the Scottish poetry community.

Meanwhile Duncan Glen published my poem *On Edwin Muir's The Grove*.

Silly Question to a Poet

Why didn't you use the word *halcyon*
instead of *kingfisher?*
Consider, will you
how kingly are kingfishers
and how very blue>
The beautiful word *halcyon*
shimmering in a dictionary
flutters its glory,
shelters in papery shade,
while the direct river narrowly
ripples with alternative meanings,
drains in blue clarity
of kingfisher days.
The hyacinth halcyon
whistles querulous
over swamped pasture
in fresh but trivial tone,
hollow as an osier,
pastel streaked with rust.
I say the kingfisher's a must
in my vocabulary,

streams in my mind
stocked with shining fishes
winding through Hardy's novels
read for the first time at sixteen
when lovers under oak trees
had a mystery they have lost.
The peace in the oxbow,
the solitary water,
the small bird's weather eye upon a bough
are more important now,
and to impress by whispering *halcyon*
is to try to gild the gold
hidden ready to gleam, already made
by artists mingling blue and brown and cream
adding and mixing in a dream
to make a flowerlike form with beady eye
upon a bush
that wings down to the ripple, a flash
for food, a rare, mysterious
and delicate magician in a wood.

Chapman: Woven by Women

On Edwin Muir's The Grove

Here's to your smothering grove.
You tarried in it lamely
while travelling lands afar,
training your blinded eyes on
a murky terrain stretching,
spreading to high horizon.
Nor was this mountaineering
or was this mountaineering?
A knapsack and a kerchief,
a folded map with trees on
and flourishes for seas on,
fresh intellectual fashions,
manna and faith for rations.

I know your smothering grove.
I seek its peopled bowers,
love skirmishing with dragons,
hunt hidden howling corners.
I do not share your feeling
of owl or eagle wheeling
above the vegetation
from heavenly lookout station.
The grove is all around us,
and you are right, it smothers,
you are so right. You found us,
the sea is all around us.

So, rhythmic theologian,
earlier, cleverer crosser
of Anglo-Scottish border,
my strangest predecessor,
for me your smothering mazes
are mumbo jumbo places,
and your strange dream creations
lamentations, incantations.
Your stories' spells must be
in my untheology.
Yet they release, unsmother
as rarely any other.
I utter them, still puzzling.
Akros

A good example of my strong response to Scottish poetry while I was immersed in reading right through the main authors, Henryson, Fergusson, MacDiarmid and so on. Edwin Muir had come from England and his wife from Germany, and his major poems impressed me a great deal. It was noticeable that all the major figures were men. Not so noticeable that there were strong cliques of insiders, exclusive graduates, and others who had no wish to see poetry extended to becoming a province of ordinary people, however well read or able they might be.

This was the background to my finding my feet in poetry again. After so much fiction and prose it was back to square one. I don't know why but I went heavily for rhyme and metre to begin with. Soon enough I was doing much more relaxed styles, but I have always been happy with rhyme. I like post-free-verse rhyme.

The Edinburgh poetry community opened out to include Donald Smith at the Netherbow, who provided an important poetry venue and published Rayne MacKinnon. Also around were Hayden Murphy, producing the last copies of his Dublin *Broadsheet* in Edinburgh, and Walter Perrie, back in the capital after his departure from Chapman. Ray Ross ran an evening course in “The Scottish Renaissance.” Alan Spence ran another writing course with Rayne MacKinnon also taking part, and the original “School of Poets” began, with Robin Bell, Tessa Ransford and others. I also met feminists and began feeling my way towards their stance.

Last Pre-Feminist Poem

I rewrote other people's poems
as Lawrence rewrote Hardy's novels,
dipping the figures in another range
of colours, my language tangential,
my irrational numbers
small talk.
They did not say, 'Where were you educated?',
'Have you got any money?',
or even, looking round my library, 'Your husband
must be intelligent.'

The absurd sound sense of these writers
so jolted my brain,
my heart (the measured pulse),
my soul (which may be others')
that I took them, at their level,
a reminder of Ruskin's word –
a man I could not have remained in a room with.

How, their introductory scribbles
derided by neighbour and wife,
did they intrude upon the cheerful party
I had set up and cooked for,
bring bluebells in, chuck stilted fuchsia,
rip carnations from buttonholes,
exposing crumpled tinfoil,
a florist's wire distorting truth?

The party is ended abruptly,
guests spluttering in taxis,
keys fumbled for, a stench
of alcohol, cigar butt, traces
of canapés and broken glass.
All the refreshing morning I swept, aired,
washed and polished solitude,
promised it a sober partnership
and set my sights on daytime visions
after moonlit journeys, making accessible
at my elbow, Lawrence, poet and novelist,
Hardy, poet and novelist, Davies,
philosopher and tramp,
oldest and best of many sparkling friends,
recommending them to fortune
and a safer existence in my brain,
who enticed me
at their level
Dreamer, devourer, tramp,
philosopher, mother,
I am also self-healing
which was their secret.

Looking for Scotland

My children were still very young, with all the running about of nursery schools and primary schools. This realistic poem appeared in the Glasgow Magazine. It is nearly thirty years old, and I couldn't find a copy, but Hamish Whyte (who edited the magazine) kindly sent me a photocopy.

Talk Out

They're silly computers, says three years.
They're not silly computers, says seven years.
Computers are only machines I say.
You're only a person, says seven years.
You're only mischief I say.
I'm a parrot says three years.
I'm in the school of parrots says three years
to an audience of seven years, cyclamen,
sea lavender, television (colour),
window on the world, mountain mist.
The light's not strong enough, I say.
It's a silly light, says seven years.
It's the only light we've got, I say.
Go'd from the sun says three years.
He's learning to say l his last letter:
learning to say light, love, limpid,
loneliness, look always, gold.
Balloon, explosion, silly.
Familiarity, life, Sally.
Where's my tea, says seven years,
In the computer I say.
Your tea is on the ceiling
says the computer.
Very funny says seven years.
Ring-a-roses says three years,
1984, 1985, says the computer
says the sun

I want my tea ring-a-roses
computers are silly
I'm a parrot says the parrot.
I'm Sally, I scream, I'm Sally.

Somehow I juggled my home life with my young children with reading poetry and going out to evening poetry events. Having always worked until then, I was entirely incapable of staying at home without outside interests. The lively and relatively open poetry community fascinated me (it was to become more open as the years went by).

I came across Rayne MacKinnon at the School of Poets. His luminous Wordsworthian poems about the solace of the countryside impressed all of us. Jenny Robertson and Tessa Ransford had befriended him when he came out of Carstairs (his story is quite well known) and later I visited him in the Royal Edinburgh Hospital where we sat in a common room reading each other's new poems. A nurse bustled in and told us: “You'll have to go. It's Creative Writing in here.”

My daughter and I both entered poems for a *Spring Fling* competition the City of Edinburgh ran. Louise won the first prize for children. Rosemary Hector, a member of the School of Poets, came top of the adults, and there were other poets there whom I knew – for example Bill Costley, a bombastic American, who spent a couple of years on the UK poetry scene. He turned up at Lark Lane, Liverpool, where I went to a small press conference one year, meeting Gerald England and Maureen Weldon in the process.

Joy Hendry and Angus Calder had heard I was going to Liverpool and summoned me to an interview in the garden of the Pear Tree Inn, where they grilled me on my suitability to “represent Scotland” at this event. I attended with children in tow, and explained I would be representing myself.

I didn't take the children to Liverpool, or to any of my poetry activities generally, though I later took them to hear Sorley Maclean, because I thought that might be something they would remember in later life.

Fable

Stepping on daisies she watched swallows.
The river flowed.
Her sandy path led through ramsons, garlic,
Buttercups and willow,
Past horses, necks stretched over hawthorn,
Across a swaying bridge
To the other side of the strong water,
And the old village.
The village frightened her. A resident
She never seemed,
Bur had tenuous connections with inhabitants
Of houses in the green.
A long-skirted woman, geese and dogs
And cartwheels round the door,
Smiled, nodded, observed, "This visitor
I have seen before."
Wetness of sycamore leaves, warmth of summer,
Whisper of bee,
The opening if all things, petal, heart,
Eggshell, pupa,
Could not quite uncurl their tongues for her.
Until they spoke
She was a ghost inspiring summer, breathing air
That made her choke.
They did speak. Stepping on many daisies
She watched swallows.
Summer had come, the path through garlic reached
The place she knows.
Her unreal steps led to the swaying bridge
Pulled down last year.
Oh what became of the summer visitor
The villagers fear?

Spirit of Edinburgh Spring Fling booklet

I hadn't learnt to write in public when I was in England. It was partly the times – there were no public writers' groups, and the only readers I had ever had were close friends.

Computers weren't there for writing in my early days. You compiled novels in ring binders, typing and retyping as you went along. My novels were (those days again) read and commented on at rare intervals, quite positively, by publishers' readers, and my poems were turned down with meant-to-be-encouraging notes from Howard Sargeant, Jon Silkin and others. I also wrote huge volumes of personal diaries, with more interesting "progress reports" on the writing I was doing. As with most of that genre, the diaries were detailed but far too private, offering many an opinion which could have had me hung, drawn and quartered, and it was a day of release when at last I bonfired them.

My first publications were a spiral-bound booklet and a School of Poets card. I helped produce a whole series of these cards by different beginners, which seemed to validate mine, in the same way that publishing other people's books and poems validates my doing my own. People photocopied from "golfball" or proportional space typewriters, or used university computers for copy, then went to a printer.

The spiral bound booklet was *Poems and Rhymes*. I'd been encouraged to do it but I fluffed both the format and the selection. The rhyming style was pushed to excess. It was duplicated on Roneo in the style of Bob Cobbing but it didn't have the confidently disestablishment stamp of his works – and the cumulative effect was uncomfortable. It is a relief that this book is now almost non-existent.

J C R Green (Aquila Press) perceptively and rather kindly wrote that it could have done with a strong editorial hand, but that it did have some good poems in it. Nevertheless to me now it seems full of fear and spectres:

In a Cold Rockery

Edelweiss
in a cold rockery
colour of ivory
dark-soiled
in a Scottish lowland

between stones
near to a wall
Seed-crusted
snow-capped
Hidden by trees
till she searches
Honey sickle
glowing like moths
under moonlight...

Villanelle
I ran away from him too many times,
through all the stages of delusion.
Now I have nothing but my singing rhymes.

Through comic paradise where the sublime's
a bright chaotic clearing in the sun
I ran away from him too many times.

Our operas were only pantomimes.
We cried and fought and even loved for fun.
Now I have nothing but my singing rhymes.

I was a hero who committed crimes,
he was a villain helping everyone:
I ran away from him too many times.

I ran through groves of oranges and limes.
I ran by rivers to the ocean.
Now I have nothing but my singing rhymes.

Up, up beyond where vegetation climbs,
down, down till there was nowhere else to run,
I ran away from him too many times.
Now I have nothing but my singing rhymes.

The tryptich card was better. I had returned from wherever I had been while compiling *Poems and Rhymes*. Folded from A4 like a restaurant menu, it boasted about ten poems and translations – there were one of Horace and two of Sorley Maclean: *The Blue Rampart*, and *An Autumn Day*, for which the great man's permission was obtained.

Luckily I didn't need to ask Horace.

It was just then that Ted Hughes was appointed Poet Laureate, and I sent him one of these cards, writing "Congratulations" on the front. I received a typewritten reply from his secretary, on which Hughes had scribbled, "Secretary, this sounds rather pinched and formal. I really did like the poems." Instead of re-doing the letter, she posted it with this endearing holograph in the margin.

Blizzard

Suddenly a blizzard descends.
My comfort holds,
built with my own hands
warm and gloveless
this side of the glass.
This is its first test.
I am in another world
than that white fury.
Stripped of its hurt
it settles, picturesque,
tearlessly invigorating.
What can I say?
I have been out there
and required shelter.
Who wouldn't?
Now the blizzard clears.
The sky sparkles.
Only by forgetting
can I go out of doors.

Poems and translations, School of Poets Card

I hadn't been in Edinburgh long when I saw Reinhard Behrens' *Clearances* in an exhibition on the Mound. I sat down and wrote this poem which was published in the Portobello Reporter. An unusual home for a poem, and I am certain this had something to do with Eric Wishart (our arts accountant). So much in artistic and literary Scotland has something to do with Eric! I was so lucky to meet such people early on.

I sent a copy of the poem to Reinhard and afterwards met him, and wrote a poem about his next big project *Naboland*. Much later Reinhard was to illustrate my book *The Bees.*

Like me, Reinhard was an immigrant to Scotland, in his case from Germany, and like me he settled in Scotland and married a Scot. He and his wife Margaret live in Pittenweem and have a major role in the Arts Festival there.

Reinhard is a beachcomber and *Clearances* was an iconic installation of hundreds of beachcombed shoes marching away from a backcloth of an image of island shores and a sailcloth.

Shoes from the Sea

Shoes from the rough icy sea
with voices chanting above,
boots of boys and men,
legions of sandals,
children crying and playing,
girls and men by the sea,
anklet and heel, tide-washed
salted uppers, the time
the tide took to sweep them
as these shoes' inhabitants
communed with shore and sky.
Who has not walked by the tide
and seen, among seaweed and wood,
a wonderful sea-washed door,
a lost canvas, serviceable,
and who has not seen sleep
in the limpets and grains
a slipper, a woman's shoe,

a plimsol, always singly?
The partner never comes
for the sea is lonely,
the shoe's owner a ghost
forever walking the sands
or wading the long tides.
Now, if I see a shoe
by the shoreline, I know it anew,
shoe from the rough icy sea
with a voice to speak and cry.

Basil Bunting was a poet I couldn't miss. For one thing, Richard Livermore kept going on about him. Richard was always writing letters (some called him Richard Lettermore) but after he had been in Italy staying with Peter Russell, he turned up on our doorstep in Edinburgh with nowhere to live, and subsequently lodged with us for a couple of years. So I stopped getting letters from him.

Apart from the question of Scots and Gaelic, one of the linguistic discoveries I made in Scotland was the variety of Englishes in use. I learned that my own poetry language was not the same as London's, and of the crucial importance of dialect and place.

There was even a women's language, ready to take hold when women broke the artificial taboo on women's poetry in England and Scotland. The bar collapsed very suddenly in the 1990's. In Scotland this was largely Liz Lochhead's doing, while we followed up by publishing dozens of women from Poetry Scotland's first issues onwards.

You could say at this point, Chambers English Dictionary edited in Edinburgh became more personally important to me than the Oxford English Dictionary. Chambers ran a word game competition one summer which I won. The prize was a copy of their dictionary and I asked them for a copy signed by the editors.

Along with Norman Nicholson, Basil Bunting was a poet of my own northern brand of English. He was a highly sound-aware poet, exploiting Pennine vowels and consonants.

The first two lines of this poem are from Bunting.

Basil's Land

The gentle Northern tongue
travel took not from me,
the Scots would not look on,
Southrons would sing wrong,
I heard in tree and dale,
beck and fell,
but only one
who used the sound well
where Yorkshire is south,
Stainmore the backbone,
opened his mouth,
made notes drip from stone
where high on the fell
a windswept tree looked out,
saw the scars of the sea,
forces, an estuary,
in his own land only
Northern mid-light,
a vocabulary of vision,
solitude, delight.

Gerald England's New Hope International:
Briggflatts Visited & Briggflatts Revisited

It was at the Christopher North House Hotel, near India Street, where I had been helping to put on some readings, that I first met Ian W King. We had asked him to take part in a reading of poets from Fife.

Ian had done several chapbooks in Scots, most of them when he was in London. I was then compiling a small booklet called *Some Sunny Intervals*. I had done a mock up and I asked Ian what price it should be. He immediately hit on a suitable price.

We had no idea then that we'd be pricing books together for decades ahead.

There weren't many copies of *Some Sunny Intervals*. It had various coloured pages and was fun. I was beginning to get the publishing bug.

I am Thinking, the poem I have chosen from *Some Sunny Intervals*, was the occasion of my first trip to Irvine to the Scottish International Open Poetry Competition event. This wonderful institution was run for many years by Henry Mair and Sam Gilliland. Each year they had an afternoon event with a reading, presentation and tea party, attended by poets from all over the country, often the world, with a regular contingent from Northern Ireland. I won a certificate for this poem. I took my young daughter, stayed at a B&B and explored what was a new part of the country to me. Edwin Morgan gave out the prizes.

Somehow I made friends with Henry and Sam, and became a regular visitor. Gerry Cambridge was usually there, and I first met Deborah Tyler-Bennett, Rowena M Love and Susan Castillo there in various years. Mair, who was more than a steel worker but that too, had met MacDiarmid in early years and even went to Russia on MacDiarmid's recommendation. Their prizes drew attention to poets outside the establishment and to women.

This free competition ended in a mixture of retirement and funding deficiencies, but it was ground breaking in its time.

I am Thinking

I am thinking how a bus stopped
in a village unknown to me,
how I walked and waited
as in Northumberland
by gravel drives
and stone gate pillars
framed in green.
I am thinking how the hills
parted by a glacier
threw long slow shadows
stolen from daytime.

I am thinking how all passed by
and I passed through,
riding, watching,
how the village
made by others
was hidden,
how the hills
made of substance,
threw forth gravel, stone
and allowed grass.
More than that,
I am wondering
whence the split, uncomprehending
fragments of soul, fell,
gravel among the people.
Was it from a great block?
Was it split by action
of grinding ice?
Is this moraine
capable of growing grass,
dear, green, sweet grass?
On a village seat
made by others,
I am thinking
on a village seat
made by others
watching the gravel,
waiting for no bus.

Opportunities for performing poetry at events in Edinburgh began to arise. At such events we needed cheap, easily produced booklets to sell or give away to our all-writer audiences. Leading a group at a *Women Live* festival, I helped write, typeset, print (by photocopier) and publish a broadsheet of women's poems in a single afternoon.

River at Oxford was written after a visit back to England.

River at Oxford
Robin and I went down to watch the boats,
past the gabled houses, the straggling hops,
over an old allotment gate,
past the scout hut, over the nettles and leaves, onto a
swaying jetty.
This, I said to Robin, is the land I left,
the land I barely knew, flat and wet,
warm and willowy. It goes all the way to London.
This is the river I was born by near Bow Bells,
river of houseboat and trout and flashing oar.
Robin said nothing. After a while we padded on,
past the fruit trees and old man's beard,
hips and haws and blackberries,
I talking unnecessarily and Robin saying nothing.
Published as an illustrated wild sheet.

It was a time of initiative by groups and individuals. There was a big open reading on Calton Hill one August. Adrian Mitchell turned up for this event, and everyone who wanted to be in it was included – it was this inclusivity that was new.

The anti-nuclear movement was still going strong and there was a popular peace movement. Elizabeth Burns and I collected a communal “Poem for Peace” by going round the pubs and venues one summer. We used four rolls of plain wallpaper, and obtained handwritten contributions from a hundred and twenty poets, well known and otherwise. You could choose which of the themed rolls you added to. Robert Urquhart the actor gave it some publicity, and presumably it still resides in the National Library of Scotland, to whom we presented it.

Meeting the Ploughman is my only poem ever to have appeared in *New Writing Scotland*. It was almost the first I sent them, and was singled out by the Scotsman reviewer. I used to worry about why I couldn't repeat my appearance in *NWS*, but to each his own shibboleth. I probably haven't sent poems in to them all that regularly after all!

Meeting the Ploughman

He has ploughed nine acres and no one notices.
The black field curls round the black wood,
crested by seagulls and a crow.
No snowdrops, nothing but is desolate.
I walk up the strip by the field's edge,
cutting a path across seasons, days and years,
plough upon olden plough, ear upon ear of wheat.
His striking blade has made me too aware
of desolation, flowering, birth, defeat,
isolate thousands who have walked as I.
He has observed on turning steady time
the nine brooding loquacious acres
alive and dead, or served and beaten-down,
ocean of fishing-birds, sky of worm,
path of passer-by, clock of the living,
larder of the surviving, He has ploughed
tremendous meagre acres, where my path
treks up and down, faces I did not see,
hoot of the owl in the wood and the land's ghost,
rhyme of the tractor-wheels, burden of hoof,
the foot, the eye, back working, shoulder, yoke,
the tractor seat, fibreglass sides and front
through which the rain that touches my long hair
and warms the soil's fresh ramps, spits to warn
the ploughman of reverberating grandeur,
slithery fear.
A woman passes by
a hedge all twigs and bramble-skeletons,
and pauses, courteous or exhausted, where the view
breathes to itself and takes flight down the hill.

New Writing Scotland

Millennial

Hard work buying and selling books, and building up our bookshop. We had started publishing with a pamphlet on bookmarks and a play. I wrote Millennial and met the Long Poem Group in England.

Sebastian Barker and William Oxley had just set up their Long Poem Group when Millennial was published, so I sent a copy to Sebastian asking if I could join. The Group had a Newsletter something like Poetry Scotland in format – our printer calls Poetry Scotland a newsletter – strengthened by being fully recorded on the internet by Douglas Clark, one of the earliest internet poetry aficionados (Gerald England being another).

One sunny morning we set off for Inverness from Edinburgh. I grabbed a letter that came through the door as we went out, and put it in my pocket. We took our favourite road off the A9 through the Sma' Glen, and stopped at the old bridge near Wade's Road. We sat beside a burn eating our breakfast. I remembered the letter, took it out of my pocket and read it. It was from Sebastian. He was charmed with the poem – it was just the sort of thing the Long Poem Group had in mind. He asked for two more copies of the book as the binding had come to bits in his hands, and he wanted one for himself and a review copy. He waffled on about members of the group, and asked me if I had ever heard of Joy Hendry or Tessa Ransford.

This innocent question had us in stitches. We rolled about on the grass helpless with mirth, and possibly triumph.

It was a great contact, and linked me back into my old London and England scene. I went to several meetings of the Long Poem Group and read with some of them at the first or second Ledbury Festival.

The English small press were kind to *Millennial* but Scottish response was muted. It went on and on, said my critics. Sebastian tried to interest Edwin Morgan in it without success. Fair enough – Scotland needed its own cultural confidence, where tides were turning in important ways.

There was still some belittling of women, and a cloud of catty obstruction hung around the cities. It took decades (and marriage to a Scot) before I was held to be an insider.

All these prejudices have eased a great deal, now Scotland has regained its confidence in such a spectacular way. Things have changed very fast.

Millennial had plenty wrong with it. But it was long, it was ambitious, it drew on my knowledge of novels and narrative, and there was a fair bit right with it, too.

Millennial, 7 (I)

Towards a country of purple ground,
rough, wilder woodland, mossy, mauve
and hung about with words, I found
a wandering lifetime's treasure trove,
flooded by sense of the profound
limitless woodland, sunwise-bound
by cliff and rugged rock surround,
sharp pinnacles collapsed to cloud
a double landscape carpet sown
earth, heather, mist or grass alone,
a prisoner on a drifting floe,
a ransomed runaway, I would go,
did, went there, casting off behind
strange half-seen visions called to mind,
scattered remnants I cannot own
locked in the past, and walked upon.
For when in this discovered land
of orange mountainside, scarred sand,
a pageant with a foreign cast
I watched meandering crowds go past,
a conquering craving told me, Stay,
merge hope, need, memory in this land
and blow the residue away.

Millennial, 7 (ii)
In a croft in the Sma' Glen
an old lady took up a pen.
The croft is now a layer of rubble
but the old lady was living then.
Now may the white burn play and bubble
and roll fresh over old trouble.
The old lady she was a Gael
her pen whittled from a cuckoo quill
the Gaelic she spoke she could not spell
so in Scots words she strove to tell
of the long trek beyond Amulree
far from the primrose kitchen yard
from the brown hares and the blue kail.
The old lady her dress and mind
narrowed through long seasons of use
to immediate practicality
allows no abstract, naught to deduce
from the black crepe and the hard rule
stocking and sentiment, wool and wool.
Flash squirrel in treeward flight,
red when the hares are turning white,
flowers spring, and the old bard
dies down yearly and takes it hard.
Places she has never been
lurk lost behind the beautiful screen
within which she has spent her years.
Cold seasons have killed her tears
for parents and brothers, tales or woe.
Bleak were the winters long ago.
The old lady has drunk her fill.
She drops her pen and the paper fades
and the pictures flicker among the shades,
Paris ghetto or Scottish hill,
palace or parlour or typing pool.
The world is empty, the earth is full.

Millennial, 9 (I)
Who makes a language finds a land.
Who finds a land may also make
a language, stating league and lake,
mapping the shore with shaking hand.
James Sowerby the Londoner
figures each hawkweed, pheasant's eye
sent from the meadow garden suburbs
by clergymen whose main concerns
are families of compositae,
devotion to Parochial ferns,
the good and godly use of herbs.
From Anglian and Dorset hedges
flock broomrape, snowdrop, snowflake, sedges,
amiable and accomplished misses
send him chamomiles for kisses,
from Darlington and Scotland, Eire,
by wild confederates, weed in hair,
minute distinction of shape and stem
guiding and inspiring them,
leagues wandered, trophies trapped, they act
like Sowerby's eyes, perceive each fact.
What would Sowerby not have done
with motorcar and telephone?
Though travelling words would overrun
the very plants they touch upon,
and travel turn the road to stone,
Sowerby plucked his fame alone
and with a draftsman's verity
he traced out for posterity
a floral grammar nature lacked
and gathered nature's names, new-mown
in perfect branches, jewelled and low.
Complete two hundred years ago,
our grey-leaved language, like a tree
bowed by the climate, gracefully

accepts its future fate, atop
its classical supremacy.
We feel it falter, sense its drop
and hear its insular creak and groan –
in that tree lodged your nest, your perch,
yours and mine, our collingual search.

Revisiting *Millennial,* I see again how the poem is about language (I subtitled it *The Far Side of English*) and specifically investigates why I had to be in Scotland to fully appreciate my own language history. Sowerby made a great plant atlas of the British Isles and for me there is a language atlas: how I heard language wherever I lived and worked.

I suspect the old lady in the Sma' Glen is related to Iain Crichton Smith's old lady, subject of several of his poems.

I was beginning to feel at home in Scotland. *Millennial* had firmly dealt with my most persistent recurring theme, in the novels I wrote in England as well as the sequences *Looking for Scotland* and *Bewick Walks to Scotland.* (I later discovered that Book Trust Scotland had these down as guide books, not poetry books, which explained why they had not listed them on my profile.) Now I could look back on my faraway experiences of poetry in England before I found my spiritual home. I even wrote a memoir called *Won't you Buy my Sweet Lavender?* which looked back to much earlier days. It is the single one of my earlier prose writings I would be willing to make available online.

Looking Back

It was a smart and pretty room,
all new, Welsh woollen honeycomb
across the narrow student's bed –
what I learnt there was never said.

The desk was shining, wide and empty
for me to pour out thoughts in plenty –
dull essays for my college marks,
and poems from my secret heart.

I never took my poems to town
to the Creative Tutor's room –
poems that were awkward, but much sweeter
for lack of a Creative Tutor.

Instead I typed and sent my lines
to distant London magazines,
like a Lady of the Town
throwing her shining violets down

to sheer neglect or crowded shelf.
Now I'm an editor myself,
I wish that one had taken pity
on that lost girl in a lost city.

I remembered this last night
when sleep put out its soothing light
and I roamed round maturer rooms
composing songs – and through the gloom

Poetry glimmered just the same
through all the changes since I came –
no fairer, costlier or worse
for shoals of schools for teaching verse.

Poetry Scotland English Diaspora Issue

That far-off city was Newcastle and the more I began to feel I belonged to Scotland, the easier it was to link back into my earlier life. I began meeting poets from Newcastle. First Kevin Cadwallender who could never decide whether he was from Tyneside or Edinburgh (and how I sympathised). Then Christopher Barnes, Katrina Porteous from Beadnell, Keith Armstrong from Durham, Ira Lightman and Valerie Laws from Newcastle. Carol Fenwick published *Howway Teesside* in her *Teesside Artists Journal*. And Geraldine Green from Cumbria, writing Cumbrian dialect.

Howway Teesside

I'll tell you Teesside –
green fields and peewits on sandy scars.
I'll tell you Teesside –
balsam sneaking up hedge and bank.
I'll tell you Teesside.
The river slides around its parishes
still with the Teesdale music in its ears,
the early primrose, the gentian,
still aware of boulders and wild rocks,
its lost gown of forestry,
even as it listens
to ranks of children laughing
from one generation to the next.
Howway, Teesside,
the home of passenger railways,
now modernised motorway,
towns clustered together, aware of the sea,
sailors and industry, tall ships and scrapyards,
villages still secluded,
hidden in the loops of becks,
banks of tall ashes, thickets
of bramble and oak.
Howway Teesside,
streets full of plain talk,
markets of merchandise,
precious possession, not quite lost –
Howway Teesside.
Teesside Artists Journal

Salzburg and Poetry Scotland

James Hogg of Salzburg University Press published my first collection of poems, Looking for Scotland (1996). This included some longer poems and sequences. Ian and I were quite busy publishing diehard books by this time, and we started publishing the broadsheet Poetry Scotland in 1997.

Angus Calder now lived almost next door to Old Grindles Bookshop, and I learnt more about poets and poetry through frequent gossips with him.

The University of Salzburg was blessed with two publisher academics: Wolfgang Görtschacher and James Hogg. They specialised in European and British poets and published critical essays on the Romantics and British poetry classics as well as contemporary work. They had an excellent eye for good disestablishment writers, a group to which I was slowly discovering I belonged. They published Peter Russell, who lived in Italy and wrote beautiful sonnets (and much other work), and Fred Beake in Bath or Bristol. Fred was in the Long Poem Group, and more recently has come up to Callander Poetry Weekend with Lucinda Carey many times.

When I first met Fred, he was complaining that "people in London" were deriding Salzburg poetry, presumably for the perennial reason, that they liked to control poetry from London cliques.

I sent a manuscript to James Hogg, and to my surprise found it speedily accepted in early 1996, and equally speedily published. Richard Livermore wrote the essay that Salzburg always required with a book of poems. He alluded to my "cheeky" quality, which I now understand, but didn't then. I busily wrote the "Memory" sequence and other poems, many of several pages' length, as James accepted or turned down various poems with a certainty that I admired. *Fishing in Gairloch* contained many comments which James Hogg said were highly interesting, on Dylan Thomas, Keats, Stevie Smith and other favourites of mine.

Oh Give Me Dreams Any Day

They speak again, like youth and daisies,
rise like religions and subside like dough
left too long, before the baking.
They catch people who are busy putting up
d-i-y extensions or demolishing
caved-in sheds. They are dreams
and memories of dreams.
I say I dreamed you were in the driving seat
and I grasped the handbrake as we careered
down the steep summer driveway in our little car.
Dreams never obey miles, or commandments.
We are their speciality. In our own garden
I look up through one birch tree summer-green
of systematic leaf and see a forest.

I call the corner by the fence a wood,
a hide where chicory-flowered artichokes
rise *en masse* with all their clones,
and dog-rose creeps out sideways for some air.
The wood is a cheat but a good cheat –
I never go so far as to call it a forest
but hedgehog and passing fox are there,
tomtit, fickle flocks of family bluetits,
and under all the humus, brittle bones,
and in the jungle treetops, butterflies.

Memory, our tea party is arranged here
as promised, on a forecast day,
clouds passing deliberately like freeway cars,
and an empty, shady house, protecting
the garden's quasi-silence, half-life, whole dream.
Memory, I am a little delirious,
a silly old lady by a basket-table
talking to no one in particular.

See what the basket holds. Flowers! Scissors! Secateurs!
And chicken-wire, obeying
strange rules of twisted hexagonals,
necessarily, unobserved. Life goes on
like a quad with nobody about in it, no stuffy
or quirky professors, fluffy professors' secretaries, clever
professors' secretaries with an eye on the chair,
no one, nothing like this, no one is there
but marooned vegetable life, a rife atmosphere
and me, though I don't count, sitting at a table.

I thought Memory was a Tragic Quean
but she turned up gay, dispensing juleps
with orange and mint in them
and pouring out anecdotes without stinting them.
I sat nodding and listening as she spoke,
aware how many jokes I was missing
but somehow, grateful for the rendezvous
and glad of her solipsistic *I-love-you.*

Dreams end how they like. But not poems,
which are not woken from. The fear
within the dream too great, or the alarm without
too loud, or the nonsense completed, all's done,
back into pleasing blackness the soul falls.
A broken poem's no good to anyone.
We ditch our broken poems, accept as made
only those that reach conclusions.
Perhaps we should value our unfinished poems
for their dreamlike qualities, Any that are finished
we should simply term *lectures* or *periods,* long
sentences
of pedagogic intent, and egotistic intention.
A poem is a dastardly invention.

O give me dreams any day, they speak again
like youth and daisies,
rise like religions and subside like dough
left too long, before the baking.
They catch people who are busy putting up
d-i-y extensions or demolishing
caved-in sheds. They are dreams
and memories of dreams.

From Memory sequence, Looking for Scotland

James Hogg kept parrots, and I have a photograph of him with his parrots. He was my first real publisher, who chose and liked my work enough to print it, and after the years in the wilderness, that meant a lot to me.

In a sense I was now an international poet, but still an unreceived one. *Looking for Scotland* got a wickedly negative review, in an issue of Zed2o that Duncan Glen unwisely gave over to mutual reviews with no editorial control. The reviewer of my book happened to be a young woman whose proposed book of poems I had recently turned down on behalf of diehard at a time when we were over-subscribed.

Every poet in the country had read the review. But the secret of survival is, of course, to survive, and to move on. Since that day I have always said and believed that reviews tell you more about the reviewer than the books reviewed.

We had taken our Brontë story to the wire with dear Giles Gordon. This took a lot of energy and time around 1994-5. In the nutshell which must suffice for now, we found what we argued was a lost novel by Charlotte Brontë which had been published by one of her friends, Mary Taylor.

The book was very nearly published by Penguin. Giles, whose death in 2003 meant deeper silence, was fully convinced, as were others in the industry, but certain vested interests closed ranks against us, and after massive initial publicity, many senior players, from Germaine Greer and Magnus Magnusson to the major institutions and libraries, suddenly became very discouraging indeed.

I never wrote poems about this story, though I felt like it at the time, but in the poems written for *Looking for Scotland* there are a few pointers. “There is no such thing as proof, there is only persuasion.”

Visions
Ten hours' hard work.
My words again are blind.
They show me nothing.
I don't mind.

Tomorrow ten minutes
may produce a gem.
Stalking ideas
and listening for them,

One's far more likely
to see a lot of grass
than the most splendid
cameleopard pass

Especially
when one's society
believes that splendid visions
cannot be.

Northwords

However, we cannot have been altogether disheartened for we started Poetry Scotland a year or two later.

The Old Poet was Hamish Henderson. It might have been others of his generation but Hamish had a special generosity. The occasion was an ill-fated poetry festival put on by a Brewery, at which everything that could go wrong went wrong. Richard Livermore, Valerie Thornton and myself, who were supposed to be the least important session, had actually got ourselves a decent audience, and we were the only ones who had, so the organiser switched our lights out, closed our room and took away our audience to listen to the main performers.

These included Aidan Andrew Dun, whose extraordinary poetry I already knew through the Long Poem Group. Aidan is a dramatic performer, and used a big blue kaftan as part of his act. About two weeks later this kaftan turned up at our shop in rather mysterious circumstances. I never did get it returned to him.

I remember Hamish as a familiar character who knew everybody. He even knew me, within a month of my arrival in Scotland. There was no condescension about him at all.

Old Poet

He sat, benign and shedding light
of years of kindness in the dim
shenanigan, at a candle end,
a flushed and guttering beacon, guiding poets
among his century's dwindling shades.
Old certainties no longer hung crowns
like awkward haloes over aphorisms,
but doubtful portents on the sidewalk
drove him to temperamental lines.
Preserve us from old men with fountain pens.
Let them go out without dimmer-
switches, let them leave warm darkness
and feminine flowery silences,
everything plural about them except
that last sight, when rhythm flickers,
when death is nearly as important
as life, and there is no more ink.

Northwords

A call went out to the Scottish poetry community for poems about “The Diaspora,” the phenomenon of emigration from Scotland. At first I thought this was something that as an incomer I couldn't do. But then I realised. What had happened to my own newly flown young family? One was on a gap year in the Seychelles, the other was in London.

The poem followed, and maybe that's about the time I began to feel really Scottish, that I was accepted, and most importantly I allowed myself to think of myself as Scottish. Welsh and English too of course. The poem was made into a poster by artist Lynda Anne Frame in the accompanying Art School project.

A Scots family

The young man, leaving by air,
a brisk wave at the turnstile,
a safe arrival on a sandy airstrip
where dawn and dusk are regular all year.

His sister, in London,
one among hordes of pretty postgraduates
picking fruit and books at Charing Cross,
not yet ready to return.

And now their parents,
suddenly not so young,
locking their car and walking down a pavement
very slowly to the polling station.

Museum of Scotland poetry project

Later I compiled a Poetry Scotland issue on the English Diaspora of English poets who had settled in Scotland. The poets included made interesting comments about their experiences. One of my favourite Poetry Scotland issues, and the only printed discussion of this topic that I know of.

My poetry network expanded quickly now I was editing the broadsheet. We asked all the good poets we met for poems, and soon built up a wide base of contributors. Typically, Iain Crichton Smith came into our bookshop to buy some thrillers. I recognised him and spoke to him and the result was poems and encouragement (including a poem in Gaelic), though sadly he died soon after I got to know him.

I had always been sensitive to the Celtic fringe. While a student I had visited Dublin, mainly because I'd read Joyce. Again I looked back:

Dublin
I loved it then and still remember
the way the city let me wander there,
the smelly Liffey and the drollery
by colonnade and bridge, establishment and square.
Embellished richness, unperturbed by poverty.
A true appreciation of Dublin
came to me early. Not yet ready
for people individually, I had come
alone and drawn, to trudge the pavement,
wondered at by the lady of the cheap hotel
but not wondered at by the old men of the pubs,
who had often seen young writers
who did not yet know themselves
but recognised the city's literary power.
Looking for Scotland

One of the useful things about editing a magazine is fellowship with other editors. So much is learnt from the other side of the desk. Peter Mortimer was editor of *Iron*, one of the strongly named Newcastle publishers (*Bloodaxe, Iron, Stand*). We had him up to read under our *Station Poetry* flag at the Fruitmarket, a perennial Edinburgh venue. In those days it was possible for a small group to get funding to bring poets up from England – we heard Sue Hubbard and Sebastian Barker in the same series. Peter and his team actually edited poems rather than just select them, and they had me do a rewrite of the end of this poem, to the satisfaction of *Iron* and myself.

Not long after this, Peter stopped *Iron Magazine* though he went on writing and publishing. One of his books was about eco-friendly burial and funerals.

The Ends of Roads
I love the ends of roads,
that peter out on proms,
circle round a teashop
closed half the year,
suddenly become private
where an old casement swings
or a jeep is parked,
turn into a dell, grassy
or a classy drive,
become 'unsuitable
for motors' and for feet –
forever await a ferry
or fail below a mountain peak.

Then when the trail runs home,
and I have driven over
a fabric of fringed ends,
blind country crossroads
angled like a web
over hillocks and bays,
cul-de-sacs, farmsteads,
a gapped wall, a frail gate –
a slight hint of trespass
hidden and overgrown
in the bright, glinting lanes –
I love their misty range
and solitude on the journey –
yet always find them strange.

Iron

Not everyone took kindly to Poetry Scotland at first, but we carried on regardless. For our third and fourth years we had Arts Council grants. After these grants evaporated we did even better. Our initial period of working to careful plans (i.e. Don't make a major mistake) developed into sailing with the wind behind us.

We continued soliciting poets we met during the often international gatherings of poets in Edinburgh, Glasgow, St Andrews and elsewhere. In this way we made contact with Les Murray, who sent us poems and agreed be our “Laureate beyond the Seas” for a while.

I have heard Murray read in Edinburgh, Glasgow, Stirling, Inverness and on Skye. When I saw him in the street on his own at St Andrews one time and went across to him, my companion said, “Do you know every poet on the planet by sight?” I replied “Only the English speaking ones!” and it was more or less true. Murray treated me as a fellow editor and inscribed one of his books to me as such.

On one occasion Les commented that he hadn't been able to find any thistles when touring Scotland. I soon had this poem:

Real Thistles

You'd have found your thistles
on motorway shoulders, in the cracks
behind barns, in small time gardens
and other town yards, and you'd have
known them from our yarns,
stamped in gold on book spines.
Cracked into crystal whisky
tumblers they soothed the inebriated
ditches, or still adorn allotments'
protesting potato trenches,
or crouch rough beside rivers.
They are banished from farms.
Fact: they are a notifiable
invasive weed: if your neighbour
lets thistles seed, you can cop him.
He must poison them or dig them up.
But they flower unstoppably in our minds,
defiant beauty in unkempt lands.

The Herald

Bewick and Callander

The sequence Bewick Walks to Scotland was written before we came to Callander. It was first published in full in NorthWords under the editorship of Angus Dunn, and subsequently by Arrowhead of Darlington. We were very busy with bookselling and publishing, and we had begun seeing the country by car.

We started the Callander Poetry gatherings as soon as we came here – an afternoon the first year, with diehard poets Colin Will, Maurice Lindsay and Rody Gorman. This led to international weekends, with Ian Blake, Maureen Weldon, Morelle Smith, Fred Beake, Les Merton and many others among the regulars.

Small Hour Dawn

My car rests in a layby
in the dawn quiet. Already
the sun, low and bright,
finds the opposite shore.

Already the forest birds
creep round the old oaks
down to the cool mossy stones
and splash in the lochside.

Already bluebells wink
and waterlily buds
float over the water
at the edge of the bay.

I eat my breakfast –
no fox or otter comes.
Twinkling tiny fish
rise for my crumbs.

Small hour dawn
lets me into its secrets.
Already I forget them
as I drive away.
Envoi

We published many paperbacks through the nineties to 2000. Some books got Arts Council grants and some didn't. In the early days when we had less to sell, I took books to London and Oxford and got them into bookshops there. As our books improved, distribution in the bigger shops became more difficult and we began looking to rural Scotland rather than England to sell our books.

We had raised the standard to coloured illustrated covers and also produced a series of plays by John Cargill Thompson, who became a regular in Old Grindles Bookshop where he would hold court for many an afternoon. Sadly he became seriously ill just before we moved to Callander and he died in 2001. We also published other plays.

In 2000, when we moved here, diehard was awarded a three year grant to produce craft bound hardbacks, but the grant was withdrawn after a year. Objections were raised by the Arts Council over the supposedly small number of books produced. This was a blow, but we managed anyway to continue our programme without their financial support.

We produced nearly three thousand of these hardbacks in all, with more than a dozen titles in the series. Three of them were books in Gaelic without English translations: by Rody Gorman, Christopher Whyte and Maoilios Caimbeul.

Poetry Scotland also continued unfunded and unbowed and has always been able to attract enough major names, and more importantly, cracking good poems, to enliven the work of the main community of Scottish and English language poets.

We had a most interesting time working with the many brilliant, exciting, often delightful, and occasionally difficult personalities we published.

We still publish books – we recently did two lovely metallic editions by Charlie Gracie and Sheena Blackhall – and we have done pamphlets too, but we are currently going slowly until the recession resolves itself. Bringing a bookshop through the hard times has been achievement enough.

The Bewick sequence was my final way of dealing with my move from England to Scotland. In following Bewick's walk I could at last see it all in context. In my version, Bewick passed through Callander with simply a word – “Callander and old Doune” – on his way back to Stirling. It was written while we lived in Edinburgh, but we had already explored the Trossachs many times.

Bewick in Newcastle

Here are my drawings and paintings of birds,
stored sheaves under the workbench, propped
behind casket or candlestick. I never stopped
adding to my notes, colours rather than words.
You see they are creased, I used them as templates.
Often would I stare at the blank horizon,
a carefully folded sheet in my grip,
as my mind took off, perhaps some quip
of Cunningham's ringing rhyme in my brain,
skylarks carolling upwards in dry air
or quick hares starting sideways in confusion.
From Kenton or from Carter bar,
from Cheviot, could I contemplate
a Scottish range to north or west
or both the Irish and the German main?
I was gated by hedged starry footpaths,
sea-coasts and meadows were mine
and westerly Wylam, wildlife seclusion,
the quiet of cottaged reaches of the Tyne.
I must speak from the young man, not from the old
not from the busy cutter of a fast-selling line
of book illustrations. It is the draftsman
in the making that I am, not yet the draftsman.

Carolyn Richardson read the Brampton poem at an Open Mic night in Brampton recently, to my delight. It goes back to a day when Ian and I stopped there after a trip to a Carlyle auction and Hadrian's Wall. I had a poem about Hadrian's Wall on the stocks for a long time, but it never came right. At Brampton we walked up the small hill of beeches, source of wood for the famous local violins.

Brampton

A country there was no room for
compressed into a town
of sophisticated music,
the magic violin –
where Scottish spirit
and English craftsmanship
collide, give life to
a box that wants to sing,
wood that trembles
as these deciduous hills.
I feel the country change, law change.
Language, as always, is debatable.

There was another poem derived from the Bewick sequence but not part of it. *White Cattle* had been one of those "stuck" poems for a long time, when I had three quarters of a poem but it would not set itself properly into its words. Often this happens when a poem is of some personal importance to me. I had driven off the A1 in Northumberland into the Chillingham landscape, and I saw these two white cattle. I completed the poem at Callander when Roger Collett and Joanna Boulter of Arrowhead were visiting. My phrase "a brace of unicorns" gave the poem its finality.

Roger and Joanna produced a handsome book and they said it sold well. They arranged a reading tour for their poets to Newcastle, London and Southampton. We read in London on Burns Night, demolishing a bottle of Malt in the process, and much fun was had.

Arrowhead declined my next offering, the text of The Bees, which proved fortunate, since Reinhard Behrens' landscape illustrations really made that book, and in the end only we could have handled its exceptional production requirements.

I enjoy driving and quite often write driving poems. I've had many adventures driving to poetry events with other poets, with Carla Jetko to Oxford, with Bashabi Fraser to Aberdeenshire, with Morelle Smith and Martha Vertreace to Inverness and with Morelle and Etta Dunn to Carlisle – to Nairn for a very small audience as huge crowds streamed out of Carol Ann Duffy's reading, but where Ian Blake's and Richie McCaffery's poems were well received and where I am always glad to meet Eileen Carney Hulme.

Carla Jetko, a Canadian, had moved from England to Mull. She knew poets in England rather than Scotland, and when I said we would launch her book at Callander she said, Then I will cook you all a banquet. And she did. She now runs a restaurant on Mull.

This motorway poem came from one of our trips to the picturesque old auctions at Montrose.

Motorway with Owl and Geese

A motorway, overwhelmed at dawn
by thousands of geese unwinding their skeins
on fields of translucent white, tea-leaves
to stir a storm, doodlebugs thudding
on pilgrimages to Ireland and Mourne,
whose wings beat three feet
above the warned wave of cobles
coasting the migration morning
of international geese, where our dawn
crosses under theirs.

A day on, our southward return
against the enticing rhythmic moon
setting a pace for language in its field-wise face
and the swing of strong wings --

the white owl lobs through the darkness
past cars' predictable pale darts
correcting the motorway's passive, unattended
calendar, its clock of ghosts.
Chapman

A few more poems directly connected with Callander. The great curling gathering *(Bonspeil)* on the Lake of Menteith was a vivid first hand experience. This poem was in the blog on my website and published with permission on Gerald England's website too. *The hazel thicket filled with wrens* was inspired by the old road between Callander and Doune.

Ghosts may be imagined, but hares are seen regularly in the flat fields near the river, especially at the Roman camp still visible after so long a time.

The Garden Sleeper is a flashback to London from the safety of Callander.

Bonspiel

Winter's black trail over the hill.
Snowy woods. Icy verges, till
near Menteith, traffic cones
mark no-go zones.

Down, past police cars, to a gate.
Curling teams spill everywhere, and yet
there's room to park.
Two hours since dark.

It's half past nine on Sunday morning.
People flock: wildlife has taken wing.
We step onto the ice,
solid, substantial space,

snow-carpeted expanse of loch,
on which we marvel, slide and walk,

where some skate.
It loves everyone's weight.

As teams sweep long rectangular runs
the click and rumble of unleashed stones begins.
The hotel's busy day
is under way.

Dogs, kids on sledges, locals, sail the breeze,
cross to the Abbey and ancient trees
one of which has collapsed
this winter past,

Abbey buildings melancholy and
two stone ruins on the small island
that cannot usually
be seen properly.

Watching again we buy burgers and tea
and pass the time of day with all and sundry
then drive away before
we freeze to the core,

sent on a one-way route round by Arnprior
bearing with us the polished life and fire
of the Bonspiel.
Stumble and try to tell.
Website, republished by Gerald England

The Hazel Thicket Filled with Wrens
Old road
hidden from the modern road
runs parallel,
shortening river bends,
its fallen stones
and gappy hedges, grass

full of ghosts,
visible in emptiness,
horses, riders,
walkers, women, boys,
sad or singing,
local or long distance,
all outlasted
by the hazel thicket
filled with wrens

Northwords

Hares in Camp

The dandelion clocks are closed.
A stir of wind will open them
and April showers will weigh them down
to wet flock, their pink hollow stems
oozing white stain like setting glue
that blackens children's hands.

Hares' bold paws bounce.
They are bound by spring
to race round acres in a ring,
to box and feint and frighten horses,
to impress their cousins, trump their mates
with poetry performances

we cannot emulate
as we lean on the wooden fence
beside our footpath, watching them
in their arena shared with gods
and Romans, this field still marked out
a playing-card game for their courses.

The Great North Road

The Garden Sleeper

He slept for years out of doors
in a garden in London, his daytime
job, some sort of writer.

I didn't know him, but my path
as a young typist must have crossed his:
not only a bright colleger

but an abandoned lover, a philosopher,
a gardener without a garden
and a loafer in cafés rode to work with me.

From my north London window also
came the peck of a typewriter,
above the tired lemon shrub trees

hemmed in by dozing cats.
Trapped among statuary
lay summer-houses all year through.

He slept behind
the throng, the push of humankind,
the escalator pit,
the tall deaf buildings
connecting squares,

mind burrowing
in sentence-stretches, bits of maps
out of the libraries, museums,
much-loved bookshops.

Leaves opened out
in a city of millions.
We read each other now.

A scrap in a plant-pot in my room
turned into a fuchsia.
Daisy-light shone by the railings.

At last, we all saw our
fought-for survivals
unfold. Each road led to another.

We do not live in London
and I have a garden
I am too old to sleep in.
Chapman

Bookselling is an integral part of our way of life as writers. Despite the increasing pressure on bookshops, we've been able to integrate our knowledge across the whole book world, to form practical judgements about what appeals to purchasers in terms of book design and content. We have sometimes been slow to deliver for economic reasons, but we are by no means the only publishers in that boat. While our distribution has varied from inspired to sketchy, we've been free of the pressures from outside finance. I won't say we've had it easy, because we have worked very hard, but we've had it fun.

The bookselling profession has more individualists than most and a very high average intelligence. Its old traditions are disappearing with the enormous changes in structure through which we have lived and worked – internet selling, production changes, high street changes, the recession itself. Buying at auction, a fascinating way of conducting business, and a basic principle of setting prices that has existed for centuries, is one of the skills we have learned to use, as is the book making and publishing that goes with the profession.

Bookselling in Edinburgh was one of the prime traditions. We saw Tim Waterstone arrive, we saw the great James Thin's go, and in the end we came to Callander, with the new communications on our side, and the chance of integrating home, garden, bindery and bookshop.

The Bees and after

I wrote The Bees in 2002, a fantasy poem of 2002 long lines, with an obvious connection to my return to the country life. I then had a great stroke of luck when Reinhard Behrens read the mss and agreed to do some illustrations for it. We delivered this major project in 2008.

The internet had begun vastly improving poetry networks by around 2000. While writing *The Bees* I was able to benefit from detailed comments from Gary Blankenship, in Washington State, US. I'd met him through Jim Bennett's email list The Poetry Kit (and I now enjoy keeping up with him on facebook). Through these email lists I learnt about revising poems, and about forms, especially haiku and related forms, and collaboratively written poems.

old white rambler rose
a lattice of black branches
melting diamonds

I wrote an article about long poems for *The Scotsman* in August 2002. In that year there was a Long Poem Competition run with the unusual purpose of using up remaining funds from the Derick Bolton Poetry Trust.

This competition coincided with my completing *The Bees. The Bees* wasn't shortlisted but Alan Jamieson's *Cutty Sark* – whatever its title was then – made it to the shortlist. It was a poem I had known about for years and privately considered *The Bees'* main rival. I published an "emergency pamphlet" of the whole of *The Bees* in extremely small print, maybe 20 or 30 copies, and gave them out at the competition event at the National Library. At which Duncan Glen patted me on the head. He was a lovely man and published poems of mine several times, but still I did not take kindly to this unconsidered head-pat. It was as though some force stronger than he were trying to keep me down.

The contest was won by James MacGonigle with a poem about mining.

I am happy to add that after many years of knowing about the poem, we published Robert Alan Jamieson's *The Cutting Down of Cutty Sark* as a special issue of Poetry Scotland.

Shortly after the competition, through my many contacts I collected enough extracts from the long poems that were entered to have a special issue of *Poetry Scotland* devoted to it. There were pieces from about twenty poems including the winner. Three of them were from women.

Women's poetry was still an issue around 2002, when I held a birthday party in an Edinburgh pub, at which 22 women poets read poems in strict order of age. They wrote their dates of birth on the back of their tickets which were destroyed afterwards. It was a brilliant reading, despite the oldest lady unexpectedly bursting into tears.

The Bees – Pre-Poem

And how should I presume
to ask you to make room
to read my rhyming screed
it is a wicked deed
and how should I explain
that when rhyme takes the rein
it takes you where it wants
and bees and elephants
with matters great and small
throng careless in its hall
and should I not despair
of getting anywhere
away from all this gloom
and how should I presume?

The Bees (pre-poem previously published online in the Eliot Hyperpoem)

A bumblebee had taken up residence in an old blacksmith's bellows outside our back door and made a nest. I watched the bumbles moving in and out of the bellows (they feature in my poem) and phoned Insect World to ask if they were dangerous.

They said there'd be maybe 25 bumblebees and they wouldn't come back to the same place next year. They didn't, but *The Bees* was begun. I wasn't a beekeeper until afterwards.

It took a long time to publish *The Bees* because of the line lengths. It was Ian Blake who said firmly that it needed illustrations. I sent it to Reinhard Behrens and by great good fortune he liked it and was able to take it on, one of his many special skills being book illustration.

Once we had those fantastic illustrations, the landscape format followed.

The Bees

Canto 4 Lines 1-28

It is as great a miracle for bees to live through winter
as if we entertained a second life
after our end in this one. Could we enter

new warmth after that last calamity, the reaper's knife?
How can the bees know spring will come, when snow
turns all their world into a woodcut: strife

between extremes, black & white, fire & water, yes & no,
the same two options that permit computers
to work so fast, where we would be so slow.

We thrive on in-betweens. We hesitate, we are transmuters
of black and white to colours, which we love.
Sleep and distraction are our trouble-shooters.

But bees don't hibernate when winter steals the scene above, or
bide away in singles like the wasps,
their cousins and their enemies. They shove

their fellows round in circles, fan their wings, emitting gasps
and strenuously work up such a heat
as saves them in their crisis. Then the clasps

on honey cells are broken, and delightedly they eat.
Were not the honey gathered in and stored,
the summer bees our yearly garden treat,

there'd be no honey in our supermarkets to afford
and none at village shops, the local kind,
from daisies, gorse and broom, or local hoard

of clover, wallflower, heather, sage and sycamore combined.
The cloudy, white or golden kind, the runny
syrupy red or bracken gold, aligned

in sparkling pots of glass, with swirling labels…

The Bees
Epilogue Lines 13-39
People and animals are like a university
senate and students, snobs who don't know whether
to hobnob with the other sets. A pity

they can't see they make up the university together,
inked not into a story but a stage.
Rustling in books – or printed in the heather –

are possibilities not nearly exhausted when a page
of history is written. One poem ends,
but writing carries on from age to age.

We poets, who know poets and have poets for our friends
take part in poetry and read each other's
present and older words, know dividends

must be repaid in life and work between sisters and brothers
and if not to our sibling peers, then God –
no lesser god of our fathers and mothers

but ours. Beyond Pandora's box and Science's beanpod,
higher and faster than the boy Jack's bean
who gave away his cow for it (how odd

if something better than a cow had grown out of the green)
science and technical accomplishment
grew up and showed us what we might have seen

before, but now excuseless face, how in their various raiment
the animals and insects, flowers, bees
all live as we live, suffer, smile, are lent

communicating moments and reflecting memories
then vanish, vanish, more of them perhaps
reflecting those lost on the dangerous breeze...

If *The Bees* was a result of living in Callander, so were a number of highland and gardening poems. We used to come all the way from Edinburgh to pick blaeberries. Now they were at our back door.

Blaeberries

Let's go pick blaeberries,
strong, dark, sweet blueberries

that lie in lairs
as though they understand
the country's dangerous.

They hide dark wine-blue hue
among mild red-green leaves,
on slopes that stalk the sun.

Let's stay an hour or so,
pretend we live like this
always, provisioning

this fruit we breakfast on,
freeze down, consume as pies,
juice thickened by heat,

sweetened with honey. Shy
on high braes in July,
blaeberries, earthy.

Let's go pick blueberries
Let's go seek, let's go early.
The Great North Road

I have written too many garden poems, but gardens and gardening are a passion of mine, almost as much as the wild countryside itself. This poem describes how we started at Callander.

New Garden

The garden's an ideal space –
huge sunny wall,
more walls of character
decked with star blue flowers,
old paeonies, late roses,
day lilies, vivid orange
geums and poppies in sun,
but ferns where a shady
border will run –
crannies and corners,
climate of water,
pure air, and the crags –
shelter and view in one.
All it needs is time,
mature plants, a plan –
cuttings and seeds,
flowering trees,
birdsong and bees,

a war on weeds,
a bucket of tools,
a place for us fools
and some rhododendrons.

published as a new year greeting card

The Sonnet is more general, though it was written in the garden of Launde Abbey, Leicestershire, a remarkable garden designed about 1800, pre-Victorian anyway. It reminded me of our first old garden at Bishopton, in County Durham.

It had Guinea Gold aconites and fabulous trees: very large witchhazels among others. Its vegetable garden however was derelict, though I heard they were getting some working parties together.

The poem was written in half an hour in that garden, but describes an ideal garden, in the platonic sense of all the gardens I have ever visited. Maurice Lindsay, another garden poet, really liked this poem.

The Sonnet in the Garden

I am a sonnet cut into a stone.
No argument so long or lyrical
has reached this garden in the past, wind-blown
or whispered by the birds, no musical
result of water bubbling down a slope,
ancient and natural, no hint of rune
or rhyme, no aphorism, timely hope
on sundial rim, no carillon or tune
from belfry. Now I live, more than a snatch
of English words, composed by man or woman
and handed on to chisellers to etch
my fourteen lines. I am a poem so human,
yet so complete in logic, truth and form
I stay here permanent in sun and storm.

Second Light Journal, and poem card

I was at Launde at a Second Light poetry week. Although I am not fully in favour of gender separated poetry, I did have a wonderful week with the other women poets, learning, listening, and gaining from the tradition. The very elderly Alice Beer was there, a name that went back a very long way for me, and Myra Schneider, and Gill McAvoy, and others I rarely or never normally see. I thoroughly enjoyed it. I wrote the next poem afterwards: I'd had some sort of dream about women poets getting on a bus.

Leading to women poets in coloured dress

I watched ants marching, fetching rose petals
in a satirical display, because
the wildlife manager was playing with them
to educate his customers, who were,

after all, comparable to the ants.
Then, through the medium of a computer,
as the ants marched back where
memory had conjured them from –

I saw my fellow humans on a ship,
a cruiser on the Panama canal.
A webcam showed them distant, then close up,
upright earthlings marooned on watercourse

and their ship seemed to me like a prison,
though perhaps they thought it luxury,
swimming pools, and decks, rails looking out,
held like the ants who could not reach the rose

without their tortuous parabola
on strings across their sky. Each one on board
could dream about eternity, though there
they thronged, assembled in their sun-hats.

So limited, yet each could tote a gun,
or wield a pencil, dictate or tap keys,
and send their abstract sentences around
their universe, communicate with others.

And I had this unusual thought,
if whimsical, the other day. What if
I climbed onto a bus in some dull city
and then the bus filled up with women poets?

Probably most of them I'd know, provided
they wrote in English. I'd know who they were
and some of them would greet me, and I them
with nods, because it was a silent bus

and we would sit, trundling through areas
each with our secret store of poetry
and unexplained or borrowed lyric,
quotations running in invisible minds

as if each had a separate travelogue,
a private loop beyond that crowded pen
of accidental passengers. We'd sit
in gaily coloured clothing, as the fashion

appealed to each woman in isolation,
each poet their own personality,
a bustling ant-town a sardonic god
could devise. A way to monitor

and say, *Look, they are all doing*
the same thing. Social instinct. It's the world
that adds the rainbow of their coats and scarves,
their sensed eternity, their strings of words.

Second Light Journal

When we came to Callander we missed the almost daily appearances of poets in our Edinburgh shop, so we decided to have a weekend when they could all come. The first two years it was just a day, then it expanded and grew with many regular poets turning up, until we couldn't have stopped it even if we had tried. One year we had a wonderful discussion of Arthurian mythology with high quality input from many different people. Another time we had a poetry reading on a boat on Loch Katrine.

Not just "a boat" but the *Lady of the Lake*, named for Scott's local poem. Being constantly asked for this poem in the season, we had printed a special "supernumerary" *Poetry Scotland* of the whole of Canto One, and gave some to the skipper of the boat.

Offering copies to the Trossachs Pier shop had the startling effect of the whole poem being subsequently published by the Association of Scottish Literary Studies at Glasgow. I've heard they sold 1500 copies. We're happy enough to still have some of our own 1500 copies left.

The various Callander Poetry Weekends led directly to my writing several poems, although the main thrust of the weekend was listening to poems from other people. "I have never been to a poetry weekend with so much poetry," wrote one participant.

Here is a poem on the the all important matter of lunch at the Callander Weekend – this time after Brian Johnstone's *Poetry and Jazz* presentation.

Chanterelles *for Larry Butler*

A slight smirr of rain
blows on and off as weather trails
among the central Scotland hills.

The poet whose tent is pitched
beneath the apple trees, is out at dawn,
crossing woods and water, slopes and rock.

Early creatures, wildfowl, siskin, jay,
red deer and roe deer, red squirrel.
Then he sees this gold, apricot scented.

No one else to claim it
he picks it, carries it in cloth
down to the Kirk Hall kitchen

where two poets converse in Gaelic,
three from Chester, two from Devon, listen
and the poetry and jazz winds down.

He asks for garlic, butter, oil.
With all the proper instruments
he improvises chanterelles for lunch.

The Honey Seller

Some poets like the crowd, others prefer to come on their own to a quiet place like Callander. Beth Junor and Richard Livermore liked to come on their own. When Beth was doing her interesting book about Valda Grieve and MacDiarmid, we were able to give her a special present of a copy of Helen Cruickshank's *Sea Buckthorn,* inscribed by Valda and a dozen other women writers, which demonstrated Valda's involvement in women's writing in her own right. Along with this book we came by the printer's type block for the same book's cover, with its title and branchy design. We still have the block.

Richard was an old house guest but when he came to Callander Poetry Weekend he booked a B&B in Strathyre by mistake. He had quite an interesting time travelling back and forth from the tiny village in post buses etc. Richard was busy with his magazine Chanticleer, which he eventually moved to the internet. We didn't always like the same poems, but that didn't matter. Here is one of mine we both liked.

End of the Sixties

The decade, departing like sun
streaked over skies with a lustre
at the end of a summer day

London full of lost property,
the trains to Europe bearing
armies of drop-outs, bisexual

in flower-covered dress,
those who stayed, scantily
stalking the shops full of paper,

gloss, terylene, candy,
their pastel record players
black plates with grooves worn flat,

media songs transferred to their brains
for ever, until they grow old.
No other decade would do it.

The dark astrologer said: This now
is the new that is going to be then.
It took years to come true.
Chanticleer

I wrote a booklet of poems on the William Burrell story. One potential publisher decided the language was too 'naked,' though it was deliberate and considered, and matched the subject. I made some copies myself in the end.

Here's the Burrell's garden at Hutton Castle. His wife's name Constance did make me wonder if this was where D. H. Lawrence got his name for Lady Chatterley … after all, Burrell was away for long periods of time.

Outside my castle
Outside my castle I have flower beds.
Not trees or lakes.
Trees don't last long enough for me
and lakes remind too much of shipping,
or death by water.

My gardener is a good man,
he tends his flowerbeds quietly
a tapestry of begonias
forget-me-nots and tulips over green -
and my wife, Constance, likes him.

Anyone who fills a place
with flair, efficiency and grace
does all a helpless human can -
we wish too much of our lifespan.
from A Burrell Tapestry

I have mentioned that I was always intrigued by Gaelic and Gaelic poetry. I suppose you could say I was in love with it. I think this is largely because my paternal grandparents were Welsh and spoke Welsh, and my father knew Welsh, but they did not impart it to me. It was a damaged side of my own language heritage. I decided I would learn Gaelic because it would be more useful here than Welsh, and then Welsh afterwards, but it was not as easy as that. I went to a Gaelic class in Edinburgh where I was suspect as being far more English than any of the other students. They were all from the Gaeltachd and knew some basic phrases which I didn't, the names of cities and the like. But I persevered. I cajoled Gaelic poets to write poems for Poetry Scotland, and I asked Rody Gorman to help as Gaelic editor with a number of early issues. Rody has been Gaelic editor to many magazines since, including NorthWords and his own Scottish Gaelic/Irish Gaelic publications.

Some Gaelic poets wouldn't send Gaelic poetry without an English translation as they did not believe *Poetry Scotland*'s subscribers would be able to read it. Some wouldn't send them at all. Aonghas MacNeacail, for instance, sent me very attractive poems in English, which were the nearest kind of poem I could find to balance a poem by Paul McCartney, published when his *Blackbird Singing* came out. Both poets were to a large extent Beat poets. But in withholding their language for its own group, these Gaelic poets did not consider the education of Scottish poets generally on the presence of Gaelic and its basic cultural behaviour.

I think we made our point. Today I would expect any Scottish poet to have a fair idea how Gaelic should be pronounced, to have some knowledge of the main writers and not to be surprised when Gaelic raises its head in passing.

This poem is a light hearted piss-take of Gaelic writing. It helped me to win the StAnza Slam one year, by getting me through into the final round where I went overboard with a more strictly performance piece.

Translation of a Non-existent Gaelic Poem

It was not in my expectation
that you would understand this poem
so here is the English:
it will not speak in your sentiments
nor sing in your heart
for it is not the full shilling,

only broken and bruised
will it hope to utter the words themselves,
roan and yellow flowers
on the dappled floor of the woods
of the dictionaries,
the bright coin of its imagery
glinting in dark hollows
where the huntsmen crooned their lament
to the four winds of meaning.

The poem fluttered past
when you were not looking for it,
because it was you yourself
that was fishing in the water for it,
it was you I saw in your boat
anchored among the rocks
where my words might be shipwrecked,
waterlogged shoals of song
off the island's lee.

It was in my expectation
you would listen to my poem's music,
that is why I wrote the bloody thing,
striving in my workshop
with quern, loom and distaff -
trying to make some sense
of those old-fashioned implements,

and it was to you I sent the email
from my croft, when the postman
couldn't get through the snowdrifts,
but I run my computer off the generator
so I can get my poems down to you
in Edinburgh or Glasgow
before I have even written them,

before I have ventured out
across the hill of experience
in the quest for the poem 's ending
so difficult of attainment –
as I sit here by my fireside
finishing my dram and my dream. *Zed 2o*

There's usually some Gaelic and Scots at the Callander Poetry Weekend. Indeed a sprinkling of other languages is welcome, for their sounds to be heard and appreciated by the poets present.

We had a memorable reading in Arabic from Iyad Hayatleh. The Gaelic mentioned in the *Chanterelles* poem was spoken by Maoilios Caimbeul and Niall O'Gallagher. Evan Jones has recently given us a little Welsh.

We've had boat trips, hill view readings, and more recently a showing of Alastair Cook's Filmpoems followed by a performance of *Split Screen*, Andy Jackson's project with Red Squirrel.

The whole event has become a happy reunion. Chester Poets come in force every year, while Fred Beake, Lucinda Carey and sometimes Les Merton turn up from Devon and Cornwall. Ian Blake from Gairloch, Eileen Carney Hulme from Forres, Juliana Geer from Berwick, Christopher Barnes, Rachel Cunniffe and others from Newcastle, Colin Will from Dunbar, and contingents from Glasgow and Edinburgh are also regulars. Elizabeth Rimmer and Jean Thewles who live nearby have taken part to the extent of having poets stay with them. Most stay in B&Bs and a few have camped in the garden. Deborah, Morelle, Larry, Sheena, I'm missing deserved names here.

Each time we all go home so happily I think we will hardly be able to repeat the event, but before long people are planning their next visit. They also suggest themes and offer performances.

Between publishing *The Bees* and this book, I've had three booklets out, which is fairly typical of what happens in a recession. Poets have to wait longer between books when customers are not buying so much across the board.

The recession has wakened writers up. There is a lot of creativity around. People are writing and performing better than ever and showing more enterprise in making a go of things themselves rather than relying on the dwindling public arts organizations to support them. We are all beginning to realise that support brings with it control and censorship. And we have the internet with all its publishing options.

Stirling and beyond

The Great North Road, 2007, a diehard pamphlet, carried more largely landscape work, while The Honey Seller, 2009, published by Tony Lewis-Jones at Firewater Press in Bristol, included several of my poems from Stirling Castle.

Barley Straw

'You bring your whole history to this moment, ' she said.
I turn a corner and walk down to a pond
beside which, in heavy soil, is a very beautiful tree
an acer, a maple turning in autumn green to red
some leaves green, some red, some brindled
and I push gently past it to place in the pond
my crushed handful of barley straw
stalks gleaned in a perfection of time
on the cut meadow's rolling edge
the harvest taken, the ground still shorn
no one by with the plough to blacken
the playfields of memory
For this straw has the property
of making the water clear
so I can see through the muddied depths
the what and why of this murkiness
this dark midway, and enlightenment
becomes possible again.
Tiny minnow I did not know were there
dart through the waterlily stems, which go down
so much further than we saw,
and pebbles bend under our vision
or hide behind waving, visible weed
before I turn and walk away
from the unimportant water
and walk back away refreshed up the hill
from the known beautiful tree
Yes, it is as she said. *from The Great North Road*

Douglas Clark lived in Bath, where he had a magnificent poetry library of his own. He had written a great deal of poetry but became tired of writing it. He was an excellent critic, and rather inclined to pessimism. He was brought up in County Durham.

He visited our Callander shop once with a friend from Dunblane, and was a Poetry Scotland subscriber for a while, then sent to say he had stopped reading poetry, but then came back to it. Later I sent him a copy of *The Bees.* "You must be so pleased," he wrote.

In his last years he took to facebook where he came across as a gentle and discerning soul, and many met him in this guise. His death was a shock although he had often been ill. He had relatives in Alloa near Stirling, and his beloved cat was sent to live with them there.

This poem was placed at the end of *The Honey Seller* by its editor, Tony Lewis-Jones. Douglas was alive then but it is a good memorial to him, and for me it is also a memorial to the musician Charlie Gillett, who also inhabited those lanes when we both went to school in Stockton-on-Tees.

Ira Lightman, who has also lived in County Durham, liked this poem and we discussed the "whale-shaped" idea. I agreed it might have something to do with Jonah, the way a child is swallowed up in his or her surroundings.

For Douglas Clark

Although we don't recall an overlap
we owned the same secret land
of County Durham,
flat, unregarded, whale-shaped,
filled with vivid pink flora
and plover ridden wastes.

A world to make what we could of
like the wider one,
a world with an underclass
of the clergy and landowners

where the length of farm tracks
and number of badger setts
height of ash trees
or thickness of Woogra Wood
were things that counted.

It is odd to think
we were children in neighbouring villages
when the memories are not of being children
but of the fresh angst of artists,
of libraries plundered,
of country words dipped deep in poet's ink.

Our bicycles upended
in the same country lanes
where we struggled with hedges
in clay and leaf-fall,
Treasure Island
under Bishopton Bridge,
or a Stillington steam-train
snorting in darkness
and the haunted interiors
of rag-rugged farms.

'Don't send me poems any more'
you said last year
but this year you said
'Send your Durham poems.
Don't forget.'
The Honey Seller

The Honey Seller was a sweet booklet with a Ceres pottery bee jug on the cover. When it sold out, Tony Lewis-Jones published it as a Firewater Press e-book, and it is enjoying a new life in that form.

I spent twelve years in Newcastle all told, so it is always a treat to visit for poetry events. I read the next poem, *Frank Graham's North Country,* at the Bridge Hotel. It is a favourite piece for its picture of North East England. It went straight into The Great North Road, and again became a favourite on poemhunter.com.

Other poetry readings in Newcastle, memorable for the journey, include driving Sandie Craigie down to the Old George Hotel in the Grassmarket, discussing poets and poetry all the way, and going with Lyn Moir to a reading at the Lit and Phil, when my car broke down on the main road near Beadnell and we had to surrender it to a garage and hitch hike. We got a lift with a deep sea diver who drove hair-raisingly fast, made up time and got us to our venue in the nick of time. Colin Will was also reading and had near given up on us.

One of my favourite venues of all is Morden Tower. It is a beautiful rounded lock-up in the old castle wall. It has an ambience of all the poets who have read there since the sixties, and is still looked after by Connie Pickard and her daughter Kathleen. I read there with Richard Livermore and Christopher Barnes. I would certainly have read *Frank Graham's North Country* there if I had written it by then.

Frank Graham's North Country

He knew the North Country
before it was knowable,
when roads hid their objects
in height, water, wood.

The names and nuances
of farmland artefacts
accent of bird and hill
and broken wall.

Wild rivers swirling
down dead-end tracks,
all secrets local,
deep in the country's soul,

Brough, Blanchland, Bellingham,
pubs round the crossroads,
clergymen with theories,
hamlets with their hold.

All were grist to him
who would travel the byways
and return to Newcastle
with discovered things

made by people for use
for themselves and others,
invented, created
dalehead fairings

or imported porcelain,
implements, crockery,
carved wood and sewn silk,
rugs, crooks, horn,

swords, farm vessels,
beakers and brooches,
indigenous pieces
of character and charm.

Frank Graham, publisher
of chapbooks and histories
travelling the dales to make
North Country knowable,

fast roads and cameras
followed him lately to
Brough, Blanchland, Bellingham.
In that rough countryside

who can lay down the law
what things are beautiful?

Antiques and furniture
high on his list,

as carpets of berries
made red spattered pathways,
as round yellow celandines
shone through the mist,

he heard the confessions
of Brough, Blanchland, Bellingham,
beckside and watercourse,
dusty dry rose,

he knew the North Country
before it was knowable,
late words spoken
by a hedge full of sloes

from The Great North Road

Frank was a memorable publisher forerunning the expansion of publishing out of London into the English regions. He published over 100 books, many on local history and architecture. He made his money from his antiques business. He was enraged by the demolition of Newcastle's Eldon Square, a fine development of Georgian houses which was torn down and replaced by the shopping arcade and bus station.

On one occasion he said to me, “I estimate there are about five million poets in the British Isles, so I won't publish poetry, but I will tell good poets how to publish their own books.”

Dunblane lies between Callander and Stirling. Because it has a railway station, Colin Will and I chose it for Poetry Scotland's 70th birthday party. Colin, Poetry Scotland's webmaster and reliable friend and adviser, and I reached our seventieth birthdays three months apart. People did indeed come by train and there was a regular poets' carriage on the return trip to Edinburgh.

A trip to Margaret Gillies Brown's family farm begins for me on the small road reaching the motorway between Doune and Dunblane, where the poem *Frost* was written. It is a poem that Margaret particularly liked. Their farm on the Carse of Gowrie has a winery and café, so anyone can visit. It is even signed from the Perth to Dundee road, where their village has its own access bridge, built in the upgrading of this once dangerous road.

Now in her eighties, Margaret is the most senior Scottish woman poet. She had booklets published by Howard Sargeant at *Outposts* way back in the 1960s, and she writes in English and Scots. She has had many poetry books published, but none by establishment presses, although you couldn't get more establishment than *Outposts* at one time. Her five books of memoirs from Argyll Publishing (there is another to come) are read widely, and are reliable, popular best sellers in her home area cities, Perth and Dundee.

I invited Margaret to become the Laureate (now Makar) of *Poetry Scotland* and she has been a tireless supporter, coming to Callander Poetry Weekend almost every year. She holds her own Stovies Night every year for writers groups from Falkirk, Perth and Dundee. Margaret also does work with Perth libraries and writers' groups. The haiku below was contributed to one of the projects to which she gives so much energy and time.

above their creased leaves
primroses shine in the woods
springtime's extra light
New Leaves New Links – Perthshire

Mirror was my contribution to a big educational project on the raised peat moss Flanders Moss, a few miles south of Callander and west of Stirling. Poets, schoolchildren and interested public all visited the Moss with wildlife wardens, and Poetry Scotland was able to publish many resulting poems.

Frost

Frost locks the landscape under sun,
silvers the gold of autumn,
deepens hollows in the fields,
sharpens shadows on the mountains,
accents the birds, owls, kestrels, buzzards
sitting on tree-stumps moodily
aware of stillness as lack of food.
Surely they must also see it as beautiful
though harsh, perhaps remember
the sun still has some hours of life
as they flap around surlily
or wait at the end of a line of molehills
for the blind morsel to rise.

Frost works its art then stops to look,
amazed that time waits for a breeze
as if the fields were an oceanscape
that might bring a fish-shoal of plenty,
glittering darlings for fieldfares,
blackberries plump again in the hedge.

We all hole ourselves up, people and birds,
for frost is bigger and scarier than us,
our enemy, it holds our ground unbidden
and we wait for it to soften, to become
accustomed here, to let up, so grasses
move and the wind blows, we have no option
but to wait, till the frost shifts,
sneaks off to its bitter home.

From The Great North Road

Mirror
Flanders Moss
I hear the water swishing down,
this equilibrium of rain.
I think of waterfalls and trees
leaves dipped with liquid weight,
river floods that rush and foam
from clouds and burns to every firth
but more, how the wet-sated moss
blinks this raised mirror full of light,
invites parched earthlings to stumble
and plowter in its star-shaped pools,
their patchy depths and aqueous animals,
their lives made possible by mist and rain
as my life has been made possible in Scotland,
this country I love for its rain.
Poets, Peat and Poetry: Flanders Moss Project

I had titled this poem *Flanders Moss*, but Chris Powici, who collected this group of poems together, asked for another title because everyone was tending to call their poem *Flanders Moss*. It has benefited from the more relevant title. Alastair Cook chose it for one of his Filmpoems and matched it to lovely water and forest floor sequences. You can find his Filmpoems on the internet. This one is Filmpoem 23.

I joined Gill Bastock's writing group at Stirling Castle when it started, and have been going there ever since. I thoroughly enjoy writing about this historic centre of Stirling, sometimes even trying to solve its puzzles. The title poem of *The Honey Seller* is one such poem, but more so *Lyndsay's Pageant*.

The Honey Seller, 1800
Under the Castle gate
bringing my store to the kitchen
I am asked to wait.
Honey shines in crocks in my basket.

The gardener wants to know, he says,
if this is a bee-skep hole.
Can we keep bees in it?
He leads me round the old bowls green,

shows me a stone-cut shallow niche.
Am I expected to explain
this is no bee ledge, but a sconce
for a graven image? Dare I be the one

to point out an older, Catholic custom
where queens and kings, and those before them
followed religions no longer approved?
Time has taught the uses of silence.

I answer: grassy slopes favour the bees,
clover in fields, thyme in the stones,
the moors of heather and shrub myrtle.
Meanwhile, I would not fetch my subjects here,

for they are outside workers, like myself.
I bring their produce to your gate.
The kitchen pays me fairly, then
hands me last time's empty crocks -

He nods. On to your business then, he says.
Today I will not stop to gossip,
but flee downhill in daylight,
back to my far-flung bees.
The Honey Seller, and Stirling Castle Exhibition

When the Castle was renovated, the large wooden plaques called the Stirling Heads were replaced with new carvings. The big question was what they had represented. What were the wooden heads meant to be, what were they for?

I found an answer in a passage of Sir David Lyndsay's poem *A Lamentatioun for Quene Magdalene.* Here's my take:

Lyndsay's Pageant

Sir David Lyndsay gives the clue,
herald and diplomat, poet who drew
plans for the pageant in '35
when Magdalene of France was still alive,
the new young wife of Scotland's King.

Excitement reigned, though not Stirling
but Edinburgh would host the plays
and pageants. We prepared to raise
wooden hoardings layered with azure
and gold, for a princess' pleasure.

But alas, that actor Death,
jealous of every happy breath
crept on the scene and took her hand
and black and grey engulfed the land.
Sir David Lyndsay folds his plans.

The thought of folk on every hand
in numbers on the Royal Mile,
free wine, free fountains, raises smiles
even in grief. They were to dress
as gods and heroes, at a guess,

forty or sixty braw tableaus.
Lyndsay's word 'disagysit' shows
how actors and guisers would be there,
in mood of happiness, to share
such atmosphere of life and frolic.

Death takes the pageant as he took
the poets listed in Dunbar's book,
but Lyndsay penned his fine lament
of Magdalene before he went,
and told us what he had intended.

The King's fortunes were soon mended.
Again he brings a Queen to wealth,
tapestry, painting, show and pelf
and this time, wooden plaques depict
the welcome pageant death had kicked

from Edinburgh. Now for all time
thanks to Lyndsay's power of rhyme,
the people's memory and tales,
the Castle's strength against all gales,
political, religious, real,

we have these pictures of the zeal
with which the Scots welcomed their Queen,
the pageant that was never seen
in Edinburgh, with all its feeling,
colours and truth, here on this ceiling.
Stirling Castle Exhibition

We continued to travel around the highlands, sometimes taking part in events and festivals, sometimes distributing *Poetry Scotland*, always enjoying the wild countryside. We often went to Ullapool, where Jean Urquhart's Ceilidh Place bookshop remains a reliable friend to Scottish publishers. We went to Aultbea to a reading by Ian Blake, Maoilios Caimbeul and others, held at the corrugated iron village hall. Inside it was full of atmosphere and candles, and a local audience discussing Gaelic poetry. The village of Gairloch helped sell out an edition of 500 poetry books by Ian Blake. We'd sent the young Drew Bain, now a highly regarded wildlife artist, to do a drawing of Gairloch for the cover.

Another village hall event was at Tyndrum, in the old, white-crofted village that crosses the main road at right angles. This time it was organized by Rowena Love and the Ayrshire Makars. We invited Iain Crichton Smith's widow, now Mrs Henderson, along from Taynault.

Once I went to Vaternish on Skye having been invited to look at some books from a Manchester poet whose son lived on a croft. I nearly didn't get there. Someone had lent me a car (I will never allow this to happen again) and the car had a fault. Its back axle broke, and precipitated me into a bog near Sligachan. The bog saved my life. I was unhurt but the car was a write off. I was given a courtesy car, the second car of the expedition that didn't belong to me, continued to Vaternish, collected the books, stayed a night with the kindly croft keepers, and drove back to Callander the next day.

The upshot was we had to take the car back to Kyle the day after that, timing the journey to come back by train.

On the Kyle of Lochalsh railway line

One of the last
single line
jointed track.

One train a day.
We wait at Kyle
on the long platform.

It has snowed
over Cuillin.
Skye Bridge looks grey.

Round by the sea
towards Loch Carron.
Boats on the shore.

Rock, sand, heather, waves
close-up.
The roomy train.

Plockton. Am Ploc.
Each little town
and station dual-named.

The true Gael and the Scot
in this wasteland
in this paradise.

Curved length of the loch.
Cuillin sparkling
white over Skye.

Miles, miles, miles
to the head of the loch
into the mainland,

vast snowy forest wastes,
the shape of our lives,
of our lives, of our lives.

The Great North Road

Aultbea

Lit from the houses,
evening sparkles grey.
Long curves cliff the dark
as we come to Aultbea.

After a wild drive,
winter picnics, deer
on roadside brae and moss,
we are at Aultbea.

Gaelic and English language poets
and local audience
from fifty miles each way,
converge upon Aultbea.

In the tin-roofed village hall
warmth and welcome,
tables and lecterns,
candles, wine and tay,

as mild late-winter waves
wash over shore sand
into the beach-stones
along beside Aultbea.

After the poetry
we dash across a sky,
Poolewe to Gairloch,
away from Aultbea,

then single-track road
rolling and turning
to a sea-coast croft home,
Aultgrishan not Aultbea.

Back south next morning
we drive most of the day,
yet Aultbea and Aultgrishan
don't seem further away.

The Great North Road

Ullapool
You know you're in Ullapool
when the little town is a sea town,
lorries roll from the docks,
a gaggle of girls buy ice-cream,
the dogs hang round gossiping
the road goes nowhere
and two old people hold hands.

You know you're in Ullapool
when the little town is a proud town,
the steamer sails for Stornoway,
the shops are stowed with locals
all saying it is 'quiet',
and a wifie on the sea-front
locks herself out of her car.

You know it is Ullapool
when everyone knows the poets,
when Inverness isn't mentioned,
when you can't find a policeman
but you couldn't possibly need one.
It is Ullapool
when you are as glad as this
you have been there today.

The Great North Road, and Poetry Library Map

Sheena Blackhall liked the Ullapool poem. When Sheena likes a poem she says "I wish I had written that." The poem is also included in the Scottish Poetry Library poetry map project.

I read poetry with Sheena Blackhall in Aberdeen at the Aberdeen Arts Centre. I think that was the same occasion as the Mither Kirk adventure. Staying at Sheena's house I met her cat, her pet rat and her daughter in law, different times. I did a workshop at Aberdeen Word Festival. Sheena plied me with poetry books she had read.

I had quite an Aberdeen phase, driving up or taking the express bus Stirling/Dundee/Aberdeen. Once I was let down by a dreaded B&B owner near the university, who booked me in and then was so rude I had to walk out. He's quite famous, apparently. Another time I stayed in a hotel by Aberdeen harbour and overnight my car was totally covered in seagull shit. I think that was when we did a Word Birds reading at Beans and Books. I stuck peacock feathers in my hair.

Sue Vickerman and Lyn Moir didn't like my Aristophanes (Hopopopoi popoi) translation so we didn't use it then, but the poem went down fine at the Hundred Poets reading in St Andrews and was included in their book.

I return Sheena's hospitality when she comes through Callander to Dhanakosa in Balquhidder every summer, and to our Poetry Weekend.

Rescue Squad *At the Mither Kirk excavations, Aberdeen, with Sheena Blackhall*

Below the granite archway
he let us stand to gaze
as rescue archaeologists
disinterred some graves.

The scholars slaved in trenches
bent on their careful tasks,
scraped around with trowel points
and wore protective masks.

The stone kists' contents
carbon date he said,
to the fifth century - long enough
to rest in peace the dead.

They had six months to dig the site
and they were moving fast.
Polite and informative,
he answered what we asked.

Meticulous to calculate,
methodical to rob.
How could he see in two such wives
poets on the job,

in two such wives with pens for knives
another rescue squad,
raking around in coffin dust
to hand them back a word.
The Great North Road

There is another way of travelling – on the internet. I have published plenty of poems on the internet but not often sent to internet magazines. This may be because I value my facebook friends so much that I don't want them also to become judges of my poems. In fact I often haven't even looked at internet magazines, but I will likely move further in that direction.

But I do share poems on the internet, to use the vocabulary of facebook. I put most of my poems on poemhunter.com after they have been published, by one method or another, elsewhere. And I have a website desktopsallye.com, which is full of all sorts of things and usually about to be revamped.

A favourite internet magazine I sometimes send to is Juliet Wilson's *Bolts of Silk*. Juliet likes short poems and I seem to write them specially for her site. At any rate if I have written a short poem I will often think of Bolts of Silk.

That moment

That moment, a deer swam the pool
crossing the river to sunlight
from oak thickets, we stood
as if stricken with awe
yet how ordinary
a part of this creature's life
to return to the herd on the brow

from some simple foraging
in sweet watermeadows, how
that moment mattered because
of where it rippled and splashed
under the ceiling of leaves
in our life
and what poetry was.
Bolts of Silk

Pond

Cats lie in squares of shade
under the chairs beside
a pond – no one to watch
when golden frogs, black toads
splash and submerge,
or fishes rise,
silver minnow, surprised.

We wait and wait
for waterlily flowers –
fat buds, like minarets
across the flat-roofed pond
in no hurry to show
their colours, or expand -
poems that remain in nub.

Bolts of Silk

The Antonine Wall poem was part of a project I was drawn into by Jim Bennett and *The Poetry Kit*, so again I did not send to the internet magazine cold. It was part of a series of place poems I wrote and rewrote several times. The Antonine Wall poem survived by being published, as sometimes happens.

The webzine *Masthead* is an Australian one which hosted Jim's project of poems by poets on *The Poetry Kit* email lists.

Antonine Wall

It scars the dullest part of Scotland,
obliterated under warehouses,
short term railways, housing schemes,
the outskirts of uncertain villages.
Or suddenly it scythes a wood,
a shocking vallum, double walled,
a stretch beside a minor road,
an earthwork, an intrusive ridge.
We never quite believed in it,
constructed to last only decades,
land-engineering that has worn
longer than those patched canals,
in places rubbish-strewn, employed to dump
ungainly memories, or vanished legions.

Masthead

Only fair to add that the Central Scotland canals have been revamped and are now fantastic. I'll end this section with a contrasting destination, Cape Wrath.

I was taken on holiday by my father with some younger members of our family in 1967. I'd been studying for my post grad librarianship in London that year, working intensively in London University Library and elsewhere, and in the summer I was near collapse. We drove round Scotland. A poem I wrote at the time was grafted into *Millennial* (*Towards a country of purple ground*, included above).

In 2007, I went to Durness and Cape Wrath again, to the John Lennon Festival in Durness. I slept in my car, subsisting on ten packs of reduced-to-clear sushi (10p each) which I took with me. I heard the ageing Quarrymen play, had tea with John Lennon's uncle in the cottage Lennon stayed in as a child, and listened to Kevin MacNeil reading with guitarist in Smoo Cave. John Cooper Clarke and Carol Ann Duffy made celebrity appearances, and Sir Peter Maxwell Davies was present and delightful – they had sent for a concert piano from Inverness for him to play at the new Durness Millennial Hall, with its John Lennon Garden on the clifftop.

It was a big festival, crowds attracted by the Lennon names (Cynthia also attended), but I afterwards heard that Yoko refused permission for the continued use of John's name.

At Cape Wrath, Michael Horovitz read from his newly published *New Waste Land*. I left some *Poetry Scotland* copies in the shelter room, and I met Daizan's friend who lives there with six springer spaniels. The spaniels bounded out. "Oh, you're the lassie from Callander," he said.

Return to Cape Wrath

A boat across the Kyle's
clear water, then a road's
determined stone,
unchanged through years,
brown braes, no trees.

Shocked by the firing range,
in fear of cliff and sea,
how could I then have plunged
south from this point and east,
beyond the dangerous coast
where many headlands march,
arched above caves
in seeming playful reach?

As long a track – twelve miles
of rough-hewn danger
and close-up beauty:
deer, eagle, in a realm
I now saw perfectly

as bridged those scarps and bluffs,
my no-man's-land
of war and emptiness,
before this tide's return,
where sparse life roofs the sea.

Pamela North Photography website

Daizan is the Buddhist name of Julian Skinner, a poet I first knew of when he was living in Wales, and who later went to Japan where he helped run a monastery. The monastery had a disastrous fire and had to be rebuilt. After other adventures, he decided to walk from the Isle of Wight to Cape Wrath. The walk was logged on the internet via telephone calls to a friend. He did this one summer over several weeks, walking though floods in the midlands and calling at Callander on his way through. He then stayed at Loch Criospal Bookshop near Durness. He proceeded to Cape Wrath and threw his stone from the Isle of Wight over the cliff, but he didn't get a day of good visibility.

He returned to Callander for the Poetry Weekend afterwards in a friend's car. Daizan now lives in London.

Although we live as far from the sea as you can be in Scotland, – Oban on the West and the Fife coast to the East – we benefit from seascapes and lochscapes everywhere. From Cape Wrath we could see both Lewis and Orkney. From Vaternish on Skye I saw dozens of flat-topped islands.

At StAnza Poetry Festival in St Andrews, one can sneak off and walk on cliff or beach. On one StAnza occasion we welcomed in a poet-manned fishing boat which had come round from Anstruther with Alan Gay, Ian Stephen and Robert Alan Jamieson (the three Scottish sailor poets) aboard, and Gwyneth Lewis waiting with us at the harbour. Then there's all the inland scenery of the lochs and glens, the forests and the waterfalls. Scotland has everything except hot weather – and you couldn't have the forests and waterfalls without the cool and rain. And the weird stuff – the rocks over Assynt, and east of Durness.

I write a lot about landscape, but I'm thinking of writing about people again. The best way of writing about people in poetry is in narrative poetry, which is not very fashionable. But long poems are fashionable, and straight people-narrative may return to fashion.

The Pass of Brander

More recent published poems have often been contributed to poetry community projects and anthologies, several published by Sheila Wakefield of Red Squirrel Press. Some are tribute poems. Then there was the sequence arising from the train derailment in dangerous conditions on the Pass of Brander one warm June evening in 2010.

In the country we've met many poets who come to Dhanakosa in Balquhidder, and through Stirling Writers, Stirling Castle Writers and Perthshire Writers. Not forgetting poets on highland trips

The poetry scene has developed a good deal in the last few years, with performance groups particularly prominent, and the bias against women lost in the mists of time. A performance poet who is also a very strong page poet, Kevin Cadwallender, started the magazine *Drey* for Red Squirrel Press. Kevin and Colin Donati asked me to write an essay for the first issue, on Sandie Craigie, the strongly political Edinburgh Scots poet whom I'd known fairly well. She died in tragic circumstances in 2006 leaving a large group of known but uncollected poems. These have still not been published, despite my essay describing them (and despite the editor amending my essay to say that publication was then imminent). I do hope to see this happen before it is too late.

After a hilarious reading on the pavement in Edinburgh late one warm evening in 2011 Edinburgh Fringe, I sent the Kathleen Raine poem to *Drey*. It was Kevin who'd got together a day-long series of fifteen minute readings at the Fringe – Callander Poetry Weekend's formula – and during the session I was in, we were drowned out by a didgeridoo in another room in the venue, the former Forest Cafe. Hence the pavement.

I encountered Kathleen Raine at the opening of the Scottish Poetry Library way back in my early years in Scotland. I had read her *Collected Poems* when they came out, and several books by and about her. I tended to agree with some that she made heavy weather of Gavin Maxwell, but at least she could out-drama him. I like to think she would have secretly agreed with (or even liked) this poem.

Kathleen Raine remembers Sandaig

I lost Gavin Maxwell's otter.
It walked out one day,
a passing scoundrel clubbed it down,
dead in a ditch it lay.

Gavin wanted travel and fear,
he wanted sex with men
in Tangier and in Agadir
where the pains of death are ten.

Our great affair was fate, not love.
His lover I'd never be,
and to prove it I refused him
when, to prove it, he once asked me.

Now I am dead and Gavin too,
we shall not meet in heaven
(this death-pain was unknown to him,
I know there are eleven).

His books sold tens of thousands,
my poetry books sold tens.
Now on the beach at Sandaig
let other lives make sense.

Now on the beach at Sandaig
let other otters run,
and on Northumberland's bleak moor
our double past be dumb. *Drey*

It was Kevin Cadwallender who thought of doing poems based on lines from Elizabeth Smart's book *By Grand Central Station I Sat Down and Wept*. I was able to give him the address of Elizabeth Smart's son Sebastian Barker, to whom he wrote asking for approval of the project. Sebastian was happy to provide some poems and a short introduction. We were given our starting quotations, we did not choose them, and everyone enjoyed the new poems that resulted in such an inspiring book.

Gently the woodsorrel and the dove

Gently the woodsorrel and the dove
evoked wide glades of memory
to share my quest across the sea,
a world-floor I could float above,
a world-bush filled with scent so fine
birds lost their minds to music, leaves
opened to flat plates in the breeze
on which lay food, and coins, and wine.

And from my carpet of woodsorrel
I importuned the gods above
to tell me if these gifts were mine,
mine to give or mine to take,
mine to pluck for true love's sake,
safe in the glade where memory shone
where the dove's mate and the flowers had gone,
and where no prize was worth the quarrel.

I ate and drank. My joy was brief.
The coins were folded in the leaf.
I wept, nor slept until I heard,
as from a wood, a dove's quiet word,
from herbs, their soothing lullabies.
'Nothing is worth a bean or shred
compared with what your true love said.'
The dove and sorrel closed my eyes.

The Poetry Library planned the next booklet for the redoubtable Edwin Morgan. I first recalled Morgan from his poem *I am the Resurrection and the Life* published in the *Times Literary Supplement* in the late 1960's. It was printed in a tabulated form and puzzled most readers at the time. All my librarian colleagues in London read the TLS only for the library job advertisements that used to appear there. It was this and another TLS item – a story about Northern Arts – that made me realise I ought to be more adventurous, so I went off to teach English in Italy for a year, and afterwards returned to Newcastle, no doubt to seek my northern destiny.

In Edinburgh I came across Eddie quite often, as poets did. He sent me some poems for the earlier issues of Poetry Scotland. He would write me encouraging little notes and was the means of our initial contact with Richard Price, for I once asked Eddie if he knew any younger poets I could invite to send us poems.

All the gossipy items in this poem happened – I think Eddie liked gossip too though I never got to know him really well as others did. I have never been much of a Glasgow person, having enough to cope with in Edinburgh and the country. Ian also knew Eddie from early days in London, and once bought him a typewriter, the portable which has been on display in the Scottish Poetry Library.

Robyn Marsack wrote to say she was glad to receive this poem, since many people had sent her prose pieces. The poems did arrive in the end, as you can see from the online facsimile of the book. They just mostly took a little longer.

I wrote the poem for Adrian Mitchell only days after Adrian's unexpected death, so had it ready when *Markings* put out a call for poems. They produced their book quickly and efficiently, apologising in the introduction that they might have missed people because it was published in a hurry. I had an interesting trip to Gatehouse of Fleet for an event for this book. Liz Lochhead who had been an old friend of Adrian and his wife was there as was Celia Mitchell herself.

There was a good gathering of poets and audience from that part of the country and great hospitality from Chrys Salt at the Bakehouse. Add to that, beautiful autumn weather for the drive through beech woods in Dumfries and Galloway and a sweet, white, silent beach on the Solway Firth.

In This Life *for Edwin Morgan*
If you were lucky enough to keep on writing
and publish poems over decades,
I heard you say that in the end
they'd start to ask you in,

to where we ultimately hold your books,
turn the big pages of A Second Life,
unpuzzle I am Rife in Zion
or take on an alternative religion.

Others will catch these leaching tales
not of obstreperousness or bravado,
but standing on a pavement with your wineglass –
a fire alarm in the middle of a dinner,

a dinner at which you were to be awarded
a joint share in a literary prize,
telling the radio reporter. 'You never know
in this life what will happen next.'

Did 'this life' mean Scotland or poetry?
Gilgamesh, time capsules, a library?
In the mind, such quiet remarks
can shed long screeds of meaning.

We, others, you. The personal pronouns
shift, mill among detailed memories.
These are the readers equal to your work.
It is a game for society.
Eddie @ ninety, Scottish Poetry Library

A Poem about Print i.m. Adrian Mitchell

'Death singles out the great, '
and as this year's low sun subsided
it singled you - and the untrodden airwaves,
the fluttering impulse of internet
and clatter of movable print locked in cases
and blocked into pages of books -
the thump on the desktop, another pamphlet,
laser printed, hand-folded and sewn
in fabled back-bedrooms of little press offices,
at the forefront of speaking and writing,
for people, by people -
and the rhythmed babble of poets
as they speak out, and write out –

All this stopped dead for you just before Christmas.
We all stopped in the week we would have stopped
anyway,
as your image and influence readjusted itself
and was seen for what it had always been –
brave exposure of lies, the music
of 'buttercups and landmines',
the shift of perception when a prophet
arrives in his own country,
in both our countries, overlong married,
permanent mutual lodgers, our languages
interwoven and melded
so we cannot untangle where one starts or ends -
the occasions, the years you spoke out for us.

It is up to us how well you are rewarded
for the hot spark of your words as they travel,
their iron.

Adrian: Markings

33 Lines for Ginsberg

Beatiest of beats let me address you
as you America. Let me bless you
charleychaplin poet that you are
like Ferlinghetti spreadeagled in air
like Sandberg in Chicago like Burroughs AWOL
as you build up your argument to howl
at the barriers and choices in all existence
your words' steam engines go the distance
freshness and fury and spirit all churned
together till somehow they have learned
to answer back as good as you get.
No one has shouted down America yet
and made America listen and pause.
You move inexorably clause by clause
explain to America where to get off
with a smile and a laff and a wave and a cough
as you smell the world 's most exciting flower.
I'd rather think of you in Morden Tower.
I like to think of you reading there
with your beat poet friends in the city where
I was trying so hard for the ordinary life,
not to be a poet and not to write,
(and about the same time in London town
Denise Levertov wandered around)
what, not be a poet, what a waste of breath,
what a crime, what a sin, what a loss, what a death
and whatever my country its state or time,
Ginsberg you gave me permission to rhyme,
for politics, passion came down to this,
the word was the sword, just word with an s,
a reason to dance and a mandate to sing,
a line to scribble and a truth to bring,
to throw your mantle over everything
Starry Rhymes

The Ginsberg booklet belongs to the new generation. Poets were pulled in quickly by facebook, yet the booklet was immediately and heavily oversubscribed, so that many more good poems were put forward than would fit in the book.

Claire Askew and Stephen Welsh hand-produced it in an attractive, collectable edition and at the hot summer evening of the Edinburgh launch it was selling really fast. Poets had come from far and wide to take part, including many whose poems were not in the final booklet but were well worth hearing on stage. In my poem I tackle my Newcastle period and how it was I managed to sidetrack my poetry life for so long.

The next three poems are from my sequence Anderson's Piano. We had been over the road to Oban through the weird and desolate Pass of Brander so many times, and looked at the old signalling system against a rockfall, known as Anderson's Piano from the engineer who devised it. When the train derailed that summer night I was galvanised and wrote this over the next few weeks. It still awaits publication, which is a pity because of its link to that particular summer. These three poems have been published separately.

Cruachan: derailed train

A rare red rose bloomed for a week in June.
Perhaps it saved the lives of those
who came unharmed from the rock-tripped train
high above deep water in Argyll
where the long loch is death's wake deep
and the wild rose blooms in a canyon,
the rare red wild June rose.

Late light of June, lasting almost
all night, they file at evening's end
in a forced trudge to Cruachan,
tracks empty and safe as houses,
this desolate dedicated railroad
five miles or more from all houses

but how lucky, here's Cruachan,
power station under the mountain
of caves and a visitor centre,
bread and soup and a small first aid box,
a flare of yellow light in the dusk,
sweet tea for the shaken driver.

Causeway, from Anderson's Piano

Exodus

An hour to check them all off the train,
held by the hand, assisted
down steep ladders to the sleepers,
forest awake and dark around them,
sixty souls safe, and guided,
emergency exodus through rockscape,
cab lamps at front and rear.

By forest, moorland, over horizons
the linked ribbons of the road
deserted and owned by the deer,
hum with a whistle of fire engines,
police, precautionary ambulances,
engineers, a Loch Awe tealady.

The jumbo carriages wait,
stuck to the landscape, wheelless,
soothed by the spirits of trees
that stalk the extravagant light,
zephyrs encouraged by the downdraft
of the morrow's helicopters.
Gutter Magazine, from Anderson's Piano

When the moon shines
When the moon shines on the loch,
on the great and strange Loch Awe,
it is white gold, is rippled,
patched quincunxes shore to shore.
Rhyme comes unbidden.
Fear could follow calm, a liaison
strange as the over-sweetness of poison.

And when the moon picks out the cut
in the Pass of Brander -- a shiver
down anyone's spine at the sight,
where perhaps a sleek otter hurries
through no man's land, where stone
is more likely to slide and move, than any life.

Where danger is multiplied
in emptiness of response,
no shelter, cover or support
as an unsympathetic owl
flies by unstirred, the cat
keeps aloof and apart, fortunately.
Pamela North Photography website.
From Anderson's Piano

Andy Jackson of Dundee was responsible for the book *Split Screen*, filled with film and TV poems. It was a masterly idea which he hammered into shape by taking a firm hold on the many individual poets who contributed. I wrote this poem overnight to Andy's subject. I am far from a film buff but I have found that however little you know about something there is always a point of latch-in. I have written before about the importance of television through the 1980s while my children were growing up.

I have been at StAnza every year since the first, when we trailed round the city with Gael Turnbull carrying some bunting and our first issue of *Poetry Scotland*. Gael was a fabulous character and he used to “busk” in Edinburgh with a variable poem generator made from a blackboard, a contraption he often stored in Grindles.

The *Split Screen* launch at StAnza 2012 was a classic, with such a happy audience and performers, and happily too the performance was recorded on film. It has become something of a cause célèbre with performances in Glasgow, Manchester, Newcastle, Norwich, Callander and even, recently, at the South Bank in London, where they did us very proud for an audience. There was Pitlochry in the snow, and we are winding up with the probably final reading at Gatehouse of Fleet. *Split Screen* is to be followed by a sequel *Double Bill,* for which I have written a poem about Torvill and Dean.

Closedown
The incunabula of television,
Crystal palace, lipstick and clipped tones,
Muffin the Mule, then finally the flicks
crammed into tubes, inferior Bibles, cloned,
invaded all our evenings. *Television*
will kill the cinema! doom-pundits cried,
erroneously. We, mesmerised, pie-eyed,
in small square post-utility sitting rooms,
witnessed the small square triumph of the box,
Stevenson's toy theatre, exaggerating life.
Coach became pumpkin at eleven o'clock,
rooms shrank, books closed, bare remnants of the plot.
Goodnight. Remember to switch off your set.
The screen collapsed into a small white dot.
Split Screen (Red Squirrel Press)

I'd just like to end by saying I have a theory about writers. I have spent my whole life fascinated by language, words and books, and have consequently read Wittgenstein and Chomsky, Shakespeare and Keats, Homer, Pindar and Plato, Virgil and Dante, Iris Murdoch, Plath and Hughes, Woolf and Joyce and Proust, Boswell, Bukowski, Betjeman and Stevie Smith, Welsh writers, Scottish writers, internet writers, comics, novels, garden books and trash, down to bookmarks and bus tickets.

Men, generally privileged men, have had the biggest profile in past times but now we reach outwards with women everywhere and literacy much more widespread. Privilege, establishment and elitism are under threat. Practically all universities have writer education programmes, but to offset uniformity, we have wonderful free spirits on the internet, Bharat Ravikumar in India to name but one.

I have believed for a long time that writers are not the most intelligent people, they are not the world's geniuses. They are simply people who have a very strong impulse for language. In fact this impulse could well be inherited, since writers are often related to one another.

Ultimately we are just eccentrics who spend our lives reading and writing. In the course of seventy years one has occupied perhaps fifty years reading books every day, and writing things regularly, sometimes very intensively. Here's a recent poem which turns on apprenticeship in art.

Creamy Fells

At Underley we swam the Lune,
a private pool above rapids
where Ann and I once swam too near
and were pulled by the river's
smooth force nearly as strong as our limbs.

Down in the river bed
mussels lived lives unlike ours,
and minnow and trout moved silently
while, in the air, peaceable birds
flew between river
and Barbon and Casterton fells.

Ann drew them,
time and again, while I sought words for them,
the creamy fells.

Gutter Magazine

As Wittgenstein and Chomsky have indicated and as the latest writers on language, such as Steven Pinker, continue to underline, language is behavioural and psychological –something people do. Song, dance and poetry are things people do, also, and the different kinds of poetry are traditions which constantly change as poets reinvent them.

Rules of language are simply observations on how groups of people manifest language. Syntax and grammar are an analysis of the fact, therefore grammar is descriptive, never prescriptive.

We writers need and rely on language in perhaps different and stronger (and stranger) ways than ordinary (normal) people. Language is not our special province. But it is everything to us, and it is all we have to give.

Literature just gets better and better with the internet. No writer need be isolated. We can publish, we can confer at all levels day or night with other writers, discovering friends with the same interests or different outlooks. We have everything to gain from e-publishing, and everything to retain from traditional books, which we can write, print, make beautiful, collect and buy. We can have far more friends than was ever thought possible before, and that perhaps is what literature was always about.

And it is about making discoveries. In *Whitby Jet*, thinking of the stone's soft carving quality, I realised this was one of the few poems that would benefit from being set centre. It also pops back to the north of England, but only for a minute. A different kind of discovery is explained in this poem about William Burrell's daughter.

1993: Girvan's new Lifeboat

Colourful, brilliant, buoyant, clean,
Girvan's new lifeboat rides in the harbour,
ready to work the coasts in the area,
brand-new, fitted with every advance.
Girvan, a major lifeboat centre.
The sea glittering, clouds scudding,
water deep dark blue.

A photocall of the Girvan lifeboat
gifted by the bequest of Miss Silvia Burrell.
There could be no stranger end to this history
nor any fitter end, as she curves round the bay,
strong and unsinkable.

A house in which ships alone
were allowed to be feminine,
and even they often neglected,
ends with a vengeance. At such times
ghosts cannot but rise, from sea and grass.

Silvia once heard her father comment
"There are few games without a return match."
Red and yellow and bright as a tapestry
on the obliging sea,
the lifeboat "Silvia Burrell" celebrates
the start of her seafaring stint.
May god bless all who sail in her.

A Burrell Tapestry

Whitby Jet

Black stone soft to carve
beads, ornament, brooches.
Stone, fine and intricate,
to wear, to revel in,
and slowly break.

Below gull torn skies
in the fishing town,
by Staithes, under quayside sails,
the sharp glitter, a dark rainbow
in booths.

Night flowering, a perennial glow
of east coast darkness, the poet-monk
Caedmon's fire.

Strings of Pearls

Finis

I couldn't recount all my poetic adventures here, though they amount to more than continuity notes between these poems. Naturally I have had difficult relationships and indeed disagreements with quite a few people, and, regarding such things as generally private, I have generally left them out. I do enjoy gossip and I have left it out in the main with some reluctance. An element of good gossip is always the cheeky, preposterous and colourful angle that might shock. In gossip we are weighing up the dramatic possibilities of things. I know this is a kind of hybrid book, and the process, I hope, isn't finished. At the same time the poems are included because they tell part of the story, I hope too that the reader enjoys it, and I will be very receptive to sensible feedback.

This book is for my son and daughter, who had to grow up against the background of some of these events, and for the poems, in a far more nebulous sense my offspring.